CONTENTS

How to Use This Guide

Group Size

Jesus the High Road Leader Study Guide is designed to be experienced in a group setting such as a Bible study, small group, or leadership training. If the gathering is large, your leader may split everyone into smaller groups of five or six people to make sure everyone has enough time to participate in discussions.

Materials Needed

Everyone in your group will need his or her own copy of this study guide, which includes the opening questions you will discuss, notes for video segments, directions for activities and discussion questions, and personal studies between sessions. You will also want a copy of the book, Jesus the High Road Leader, which provides further insights into the material you are covering in this study. To aid your study experience, you will be encouraged to make sure you've read specific chapters in the book to prepare for the group's next meeting.

Facilitation

Your group will need to appoint a person to serve as a facilitator. This person will be responsible for starting the video and keeping track of time during discussions and activities. Facilitators may also read questions aloud and monitor discussions, prompting participants to respond and assuring that everyone has the opportunity to participate. If you have been chosen for this role, note there are additional instructions and resources in the back of this guide to help you lead your group members through the study.

Personal Studies

During the week, you can maximize the impact of the course with the personal studies provided for each session. You can treat each personal study section like a devotional and use them in whatever way works best for your schedule. You could do one section each day for three days of the week or complete them all in one sitting. These personal studies are not intended to be burdensome or time-consuming but to provide a richer experience and continuity in between your group sessions.

INTRODUCTION

> "WHEN WE TAKE THE HIGH ROAD, WE LOVE AND VALUE PEOPLE THE WAY JESUS DID." — JESUS THE HIGH ROAD LEADER, PAGE 19

The life of Jesus provides a model of leadership unlike any other. Whether healing the sick, confronting religious leaders, washing people's feet, or going to the cross, Jesus embraced God's values and lived them out perfectly. His life embodies the perfect example of servant leadership. As his followers, we're called to make the same kind of positive difference in the lives of others, to be salt and light in the world around us.

As our world experiences a crisis in leadership, the example set by Jesus remains as timeless and relevant as ever. Too many leaders devalue people who are not like them and fail to live out the values exemplified by Jesus.

Sadly, this happens even in the church. Many of us have become distracted and placed our hope in government and human laws to bring about a better life for us. Even worse, we put our hope in elected leaders of both parties who don't embrace the values of Jesus. Many of these leaders lack civility, lack authenticity, divide the people, place themselves and their party above everyone else, keep score, and get even with others when they lose. They have no idea how to be a servant leader.

Considering how to lead, we find there are essentially only three paths we can walk in life: People on the low road selfishly take more than they give and instead of making the world better and brighter, they make the world worse and darker. People on the middle road focus on fairness and score-keeping, sustaining the status quo without ever making things better or brighter. People on the high road follow the example of Jesus, giving more than they take, serving others out of love, turning the other cheek, and bringing others together. These people lead others to Jesus, and in the process, make the world better and brighter.

Jesus challenged his followers to make sacrifices to serve others, rather than expecting others to sacrifice or serve them. He said, "Whoever wants to be my disciple must deny themselves and take up their cross daily and follow me. For whoever wants to save their life will lose it, but whoever loses their life for me will save it" (Luke 9:23–24). As our perfect high-road leader, Jesus expects us to live out high-road behavior with others in everything we do.

Our role as Christians is to help people connect with God. It's not possible to do that if we continually draw lines, argue with people, and build walls between us and them. Jesus came to this earth to be on common ground with us so he could connect us with God. As his chosen representatives, we must do the same.

When we take the high road, we love and value people the way Jesus did. That will make us look at people with whom we disagree in a different light. As people who have been saved by grace, we know that only Jesus can cure the human heart. And that is the message we need to pass on to others. How do we best do that? By following Jesus, our high-road leader.

As a companion to our book Jesus the High Road Leader, this study guide explores eight behaviors Jesus modeled that show you how to be salt and light to others. Only Jesus can infuse your leadership with something that attracts those who don't know God. Only by following Jesus on the high road in a low-road world will people want to know why you're different. If you want to lead people to Jesus, then you must walk the high road where Jesus travels.

CHECKING IN

Consider the following questions about what and who has influenced your present understanding of leadership. If you're part of a group study, introduce yourselves and discuss your responses.

- What are some of the various leadership models you've observed or tried to follow? Which ones appeal to you most? Why?

- Who are a couple of the leaders you most admire? Which aspects of their leadership do you aspire to emulate? Why?

HEARING THE WORD

Jesus demonstrated high-road leadership in everything he did and said. Read the following passage in which he explains the importance of being salt and light in how we live and lead. If in a group, have someone read the passage aloud before answering the questions that follow.

"You are the salt of the earth. But if the salt loses its saltiness, how can it be made salty again? It is no longer good for anything, except to be thrown out and trampled underfoot.

"You are the light of the world. A town built on a hill cannot be hidden. Neither do people light a lamp and put it under a bowl. Instead they put it on its stand, and it gives light to everyone in the house. In the same way, let your light shine before others, that they may see your good deeds and glorify your Father in heaven.

MATTHEW 5:13–16

- Why do you suppose Jesus chose these two particular comparisons when addressing his followers? How do they convey the impact we have when we follow his example?

- What are some ways you often offer salt and light to those around you? How does the way you interact with people reflect your relationship with Jesus?

TAKING THE HIGH ROAD

Knowing that Jesus took the high road with everyone, and knowing he wants you to follow his example, you have a choice to make about how you will lead. As you follow in Jesus' footsteps, you realize that your daily decisions reflect the core values of your soul. The spiritual values you use as the basis for how you behave and relate to others shapes the culture around us. As someone who has been saved by grace, you know that only Jesus can satisfy the human heart. This is the message you're called to pass on to others. And the best way to do this is by following Jesus, the ultimate high-road leader.

- What are some of the values you hold that form the basis for how you live and lead? How did these values become part of your life?

- How would you describe the differences between a high-road leader and a low-road leader? Between a middle-road leader?

- When have you taken a low-road or middle-road leadership direction rather than the high road? What factors contributed to your decisions and actions?

- How does increasing your awareness of the way Jesus chose the high road help you follow his example in your daily life?

- How does following Jesus' example impact those around you? How does the way you lead and relate to others reflect their understanding of who God is?

LEADING LIKE JESUS

In the space below, complete the following sentences as you consider your goals, expectations, and intentions for completing this study of Jesus the High Road Leader. Choose one of them to share in your group as you wrap up your time together.

What I hope to get from completing this study of Jesus as the perfect high-road leader is...

I want to follow the example of Jesus as a high-road leader because...

CLOSING IN PRAYER

Spend a few moments in prayer, reflecting on how you would like to grow by completing this study. Go around the group and share any personal prayer requests you would like others to pray about, and then pray for those requests together, either silently or out loud or both. Thank God for bringing you all together to focus on being a high-road leader like Jesus. Ask him to inspire and empower you as you go through this study together.

BEFORE NEXT TIME

If you haven't already started reading Jesus the High Road Leader by John C. Maxwell and Chris Hodges, then now is a great time to begin. Before the next session, read or review Chapter 1, "What Road Will You Take?", and Chapter 2, "Jesus Valued All People."

SESSION 1
JESUS VALUED ALL PEOPLE

Jesus saw people differently than others. He looked beyond their problems and saw their potential.

Jesus the High Road Leader, page 25

GETTING STARTED

God loves and values people—all people—so much that he gave his only Son, Jesus, so that anyone can have a whole and lasting life. Fulfilling God's desire for everyone to be saved, Jesus didn't condemn people but offered them freedom from sin. As the ultimate high-road leader, Jesus assumed the best in people and treated them with love and respect.

While so many people compare, compete against, and condemn those they consider unworthy, Jesus valued everyone. He was always for the "outsiders," always looking for the one who was overlooked, seeing potential in those who seemingly had little to offer. Jesus valued others based upon who he was, not who they were or what they had done. No one had to be a friend or even good to be loved by Jesus.

The life of Jesus, the high-road leader, offers hope to people. The Scriptures are filled with hope offered to people who have none. Why? Because Jesus loves us—all of us. If we as Christians separate ourselves from lost people, we become more likely to judge them. We need to remember that God doesn't ask us to change to accept us. He accepts us so he can change us! Accepting people where they are creates a common ground, and the road between others and Jesus is common ground, not a battleground.

Follow the footsteps of Jesus throughout the Gospels, and you will conclude that Jesus did not follow social and cultural labels of people. He chose fishermen as disciples, dined with tax collectors, healed lepers, forgave a woman caught in adultery, and engaged in conversation with a Samaritan woman. As Christ's followers and ambassadors, we need to value everyone enough to reach out to them when they fall and lift them back up again. Following his example of loving and valuing all people, we see past others' sins and see the value Jesus sees in them.

CHECKING IN

For this first session, go around the group and introduce yourselves as you answer one of the following questions:

- What are some ways our culture assesses the value of people? What's the basis for those who are valued most? Least?

- When have you been viewed as valuable by certain people? What determined your value?

HEARING THE WORD

Have someone read aloud the following passage about the greatest commandments according to Jesus.

Hearing that Jesus had silenced the Sadducees, the Pharisees got together. One of them, an expert in the law, tested him with this question: "Teacher, which is the greatest commandment in the Law?"

Jesus replied: "'Love the Lord your God with all your heart and with all your soul and with all your mind.' This is the first and greatest commandment.And the second is like it: 'Love your neighbor as yourself.' All the Law and the Prophets hang on these two commandments."
Matthew 22:34–40

Now, pair up with the person next to you and share your answers to the following questions:

- How does Jesus' response reflect the way he values all people?

- How do both commandments here reflect the way God values everyone?

TAKING THE HIGH ROAD

Play the video segment for session 1. Use the space on the next page to jot down the big ideas that stand out to you. Then take a few minutes with your group members to discuss what you just watched and explore these concepts in Scripture.

- What word, phrase, or image lingers with you from the poem that John read? In this poem, how does John describe high-road leadership?

- How can applying John's three-dimensional approach—looking at your perspective, God's perspective in Scripture, and others' perspective—enhance your understanding and application of the eight distinctives of high-road leadership?

- Based on who Jesus chose as his disciples, what can we learn about the way he valued their differences? Why do you suppose Jesus chose these men rather than others that we might consider better qualified?

- Who are the "neighbors" you struggle to love and respect the way Jesus does? What makes it challenging for you to value them as God values them?

- As you consider the various outsiders and outcasts Jesus encountered, which one particularly stands out or resonates with you right now? How does knowing that Jesus values you the same way empower you to value others?

NOTES

LEADING LIKE JESUS

As this session winds down, complete the following short activity on your own.

Briefly review the video teaching notes you took or comments you made. Reflect for a moment on the group discussion you just had. Write down any questions you want to answer or thoughts you want to explore further. Underline or circle anything you want to make sure you remember and reflect on prior to your next group session.

In the space below, complete the following sentences as you consider what you will take away from this session—including the teaching, activities, and discussions.

- What I want to remember from this session is...

- One way I want to improve on valuing people the way Jesus values them is...

CLOSING IN PRAYER

Go around the group and share any personal prayer requests you would like others to pray about, and then pray for those requests together, either silently or out loud or both. Thank God for the way he loves and values all people, including each member of your group. Ask him to show you how you can love and value people the same way Jesus did.

BEFORE NEXT TIME

Before the next session, read and reflect on Chapter 3, "Jesus Gave More Than He Took," in Jesus the High Road Leader, and begin thinking about what's required for you to follow his example and give more than you take.

Between-Sessions Personal Study

The questions and exercises provided in this section are designed to help you receive the greatest benefit from reading the book and applying it to your own life. This section is not intended to be burdensome or add pressure but simply to enhance your growth as a high-road leader like Jesus. There will be time for you to share some of your responses and reflections at the beginning of the next group session. Begin with a few moments of silent prayer, stilling your heart before God and asking his Spirit to guide you as you engage with this study.

Choosing the High Road

Jesus, our high-road leader, expects us to live out high-road behavior with others in everything we do. Our world is filled with people who live on the low road. That's understandable because our world is filled with sin and darkness. What kind of ambassadors are we if our actions and values as Christians are the same as those who have no relationship with God? Similarly, if we choose the middle road and just settle for the status quo, we're not making a difference to bring light to this dark world. As believers committed to following Jesus, we are his ambassadors, representing him in everything we say or do (2 Cor. 5:19–20). We no longer have the freedom of going our own way or expressing our own message. Obeying our high-road leader Jesus, we share his message of reconciliation between God and people.

We are not just ambassadors of Christ—we are chosen to do priestly work. Writing to believers in the early church, Peter explained:

But you are the ones chosen by God, chosen for the high calling of priestly work, chosen to be a holy people, God's instruments to do his work and speak out for him, to tell others of the night-and-day difference he made for you—from nothing to something, from rejected to accepted. Friends, this world is not your home, so don't make yourselves cozy in it. Don't indulge your ego at the expense of your soul. Live an exemplary life in your neighborhood so that your actions will refute their prejudices. Then they'll be won over to God's side and be there to join in the celebration when he arrives.
1 Peter 2:9–12, MSG

Our ultimate goal as high-road leaders who follow Jesus is simple: to help people connect with God. It's not possible to do that if we continually draw lines, argue with people, and build walls between us and them. Jesus came to this earth to be on common ground with us so he could connect us with God. As his chosen representatives, we must do the same.

When we take the high road, we love and value people the way Jesus did. That way of thinking will make us look at people with whom we disagree in a different light. We no longer assess their value according to worldly standards and labels; we value them as people created in the image of God, just as we are, and love them accordingly.

Knowing that Jesus took the high road with everyone, and knowing he wants you to follow his example, you have a choice to make. Being a high-road leader like Jesus requires you to follow an intentional path. Will you follow in his footsteps? Will you embrace all of Jesus' values? Your values are more than just decisions; they are your soul. The values you live determine how you behave and how our world will function—regardless of the laws made or expectations held. Matters of the heart will never be solved with legislative action or popular opinion. They require the love of God and his free gift of salvation through the sacrifice Jesus made on the cross.

As people who have been saved by grace, we know that only Jesus can cure the human heart. And that is the message we need to pass on to others. How do we best do that? By following Jesus, our high-road leader.

- On a scale of 1 to 10, with 1 being "lowest" and 10 being "highest," what score reflects your commitment to do whatever it takes to follow the example of Jesus, the ultimate high-road leader? What has stood in the way of following his example in the past? How will you overcome these obstacles going forward?

- What comes to mind when you think of the role of an ambassador in global relations? How does this role compare to what you're called to do as Christ's ambassador?

- What is significant about being called to do "priestly work" as "God's instrument"? What specific priestly work has God called you to do in your present season of life?

- How can the way you value people help connect them to God? Why is valuing others the way Jesus values them such an important part of being a high-road leader?

- When have you recently needed to check your ego or set aside your personal agenda in order to focus on following the example of Jesus? What did you learn from this experience?

LEADING BY GOD'S WORD

Just as Jesus exemplifies the ultimate high-road leader, God's Word serves as the ultimate guide to high-road leadership. We're told, "All Scripture is God-breathed and is useful for teaching, rebuking, correcting and training in righteousness, so that the servant of God may be thoroughly equipped for every good work" [2 Tim. 3:16–17]. If you want to grow more like Jesus, then spending time in the Bible will draw you closer in your relationship to him.

There, you will find instruction, guidance, wisdom, and assurance as well as stories of the faithful. In the pages of the Gospels, you can study the life of Jesus, the greatest high-road leader. In particular, you can witness how Jesus demonstrated timeless high-road principles that you can continue to apply and practice today.

In all his interactions with others, Jesus showed people a kind of love and respect that ran counter to cultural, social, religious and political customs and traditions. He did not treat them according to their class, gender, ethnicity, status, or wealth. He saw them as individuals, as men and women made by the Father in his own divine image.

Jesus looked beyond their appearance and into their hearts. He looked beyond their problems and saw their potential. Most people see others with their shortcomings, weaknesses, mistakes, and baggage and label them, assuming they won't or can't change. Jesus, however, looked beyond their problems and saw their possibilities. He valued them accordingly and helped them see what he saw in them.

We see this illustrated in one of the best known parables Jesus told: The Good Samaritan. Luke recounts a discussion about the greatest commandment between Jesus and an expert in the law. Hoping to narrow down the list of who he might be expected to love, the expert asked Jesus to define who he meant by neighbor. To help this man see the importance of valuing all people, Jesus then told this story:

"A man was going down from Jerusalem to Jericho, when he was attacked by robbers. They stripped him of his clothes, beat him and went away, leaving him half dead. A priest happened to be going down the same road, and when he saw the man, he passed by on the other side. So too, a Levite, when he came to the place and saw him, passed by on the other side. But a Samaritan, as he traveled, came where the man was; and when he saw him, he took pity on him. He went to him and bandaged his wounds, pouring on oil and wine. Then he put the man on his own donkey, brought him to an inn and took care of him. The next day he took out two denarii and gave them to the innkeeper. 'Look after him,' he said, 'and when I return, I will reimburse you for any extra expense you may have.'
"Which of these three do you think was a neighbor to the man who fell into the hands of robbers?"
The expert in the law replied, "The one who had mercy on him."
Jesus told him, "Go and do likewise."
Luke 10:30–37

Why would Jesus choose to illustrate this story using a Samaritan? Because his Jewish audience would have seen a Samaritan as a political, spiritual, and racial enemy—someone generally despised. Jesus, in contrast, saw him as someone of value. And Jesus wanted his followers to be like him. We are to go out of our way and pay a price for others, like the Good Samaritan. In other words, we are to find people who are beat up, who have fallen, who are broken, and we are to restore them.

Jesus gave his life to restore us, and he gave this example to encourage us to restore others.
We will do that only if we value them.

- What are some of the biblical principles that have shaped your leadership style?
  How has Jesus served as your model of a servant leader in the past?

- How quickly do you usually form impressions of new people you meet?
  What informs your conclusions about the kind of person they are?

- What stands out most to you in the parable of the Good Samaritan? Why?

- When have you been too busy to notice the needs of others around you? What's required for you to slow down and be more aware of those you can serve?

- If you were going to update this parable with contemporary details, who would you choose in the role of the Samaritan? Why?

WALKING THE HIGH ROAD

One of the greatest challenges to valuing people the way Jesus values them comes from within. In your group session, you read aloud the passage from Matthew in which Jesus cites the two greatest commandments, to love God with all your heart and soul and mind (Matt. 22:37) and to love your neighbor as yourself (Matt. 22:39). The second commandment sounds clear enough because nearly all human beings tend to their own self-interests. Our sinful nature predisposes us to put ourselves above others.

Living in a fallen world, however, can also cause us to struggle with seeing ourselves clearly. We have suffered injuries, physical as well as emotional, that leave scars and prevent us from viewing ourselves the way God sees us. He created us and knows us better than we know ourselves, but sometimes we accept the labels others place on us and make false assumptions about who we are.

Unfortunately, many people compensate for these inaccurate, negative views of themselves by adopting a "one up" or "one down" mindset. They either look for ways to elevate themselves through their attributes and accomplishments while putting others down, or they lower their self-worth and consider themselves inferior to others around them. Tilting toward either extreme pulls us away from the truth of knowing our true identity in Christ.

When you don't know who God says you are or fail to live out that identity, then you will likely struggle to value other people. If you can't love yourself as God loves you, then it's hard to love your neighbor as yourself. In order to follow the example Jesus set for valuing people, you may need to consider how much he values you.

Here's what is true: God loves you more than you love yourself. He values you more than you value yourself. He also encourages you more than you encourage yourself. For anything negative that you can say to yourself, God has a positive response for you. We see this demonstrated by the way Jesus offered hope to people. The Scriptures are filled with hope offered to people who have none. Why? Because Jesus, our high-road Leader, loves us—all of us.

Read through the following sound bites of self-talk, which are often negative and inaccurate, as compared to what is true based on God's Word. Then answer the questions and complete the exercises that follow.

You say: It's impossible.
God says: All things are possible. (Luke 18:27)

You say: I'm too tired.
God says: I will give you rest. (Matt. 11:28–30)

You say: Nobody really loves me.
God says: I love you. (John 3:16 and John 13:34)

You say: I can't go on.
God says: My grace is sufficient. (2 Cor. 12:9)

You say: I can't figure things out.
God says: I will direct your steps. (Prov. 3:5–6)

You say: I can't do it.
God says: You can do all things. (Phil. 4:13)

You say: I'm not able.
God says: I am able. (2 Cor. 9:8)

You say: It's not worth it.
God says: I will be worth it. (Rom. 8:28)

You say: I can't forgive myself.
God says: I forgive you. (1 John 1:9 and Rom. 8:1)

You say: I can't manage.
God says: I will supply all your needs. (Phil. 4:19)

You say: I'm afraid.
God says: I have not given you a spirit of fear. (2 Tim. 1:7)

You say: I'm always worried and frustrated.
God says: Cast all your cares on me. (1 Peter 5:7)

You say: I'm not smart enough.
God says: I give you wisdom. (1 Cor. 1:30)

You say: I feel all alone.
God says: I will never leave you or forsake you. (Heb. 13:5)

- Have you ever considered that you might struggle with loving and valuing others because of the way you struggle to love and value yourself? When have you noticed this connection?

- What are some of the assumptions you often make about others that reflect your own struggles with self-confidence and self-worth? How does this come out in the way you treat others?

- Look through the list above, comparing what you say with what God says. Place a check mark or star next to the ones that especially hit home with you. Which of these do you battle most frequently? How have these false views limited your ability to be a high-road leader?

- Choose one pair you marked as a struggle for you and look up the Bible verse reflecting what God says is true. Write it out in the space below. Make it your goal to memorize this verse before your next group meeting. Practice calling it to mind every time you find yourself thinking anything other than what God says is true.

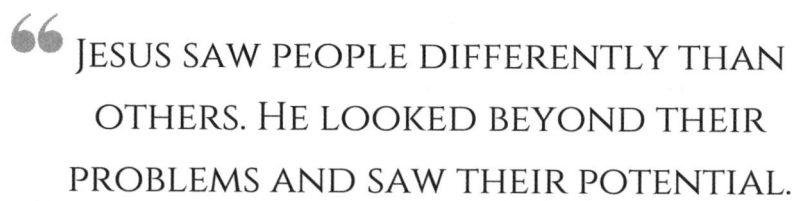

"JESUS SAW PEOPLE DIFFERENTLY THAN OTHERS. HE LOOKED BEYOND THEIR PROBLEMS AND SAW THEIR POTENTIAL.

JESUS THE HIGH ROAD LEADER, PAGE 25

SESSION 2
Jesus Gave More Than He Took

The value of your life isn't determined by how much you achieve or accumulate but by how much of your life you give away.

Jesus the High Road Leader, page 45

Getting Started

When Jesus is the model for your calling as a high-road leader, you learn to give more than you take. His example requires you to put those you serve ahead of yourself and give them all you can without expecting anything in return. Jesus embodies high-road leadership by humbling himself and loving others unconditionally.

In fact, the very first miracle Jesus performed—turning water into wine at a wedding in Cana (John 2:1–12)—displays his unmerited generosity. Rather than allow the bride and groom to suffer extreme embarrassment during their joyous celebration, Jesus stepped up to provide the ultimate wedding gift. His quiet intervention not only prevented their humiliation but blessed them as well as everyone in attendance. The divine generosity of Jesus exceeded human abilities.

This divine generosity reflects the unconditional love Jesus has for all people as well as the love of his Father who sent him. "For God so loved the world that he gave his one and only Son" (John 3:16). God loved human beings so much that he made the ultimate sacrifice. Motivated and empowered by this same heavenly love, Jesus was willing to suffer and die on the cross in order to restore relationship between God and all people.

Giving more than you take exemplifies the very heart of Jesus as a high-road leader. He told his followers, "So the last will be first, and the first will be last" (Matt. 20:16). This kind of selfless leadership does not try to get ahead and take all the credit; this kind of high-road leadership serves others without requiring attention. God's Word confirms this: "Do nothing out of selfish ambition or vain conceit. Rather, in humility value others above yourselves, not looking to your own interests but each of you to the interests of others" (Phil. 2:3-4).

Giving more than you take is at the core of taking the high road and being a servant leader like Jesus. This value provides the soil in which all the other high-road values grow and flourish, yielding a heart that gives and a hand that is open.

CHECKING IN

Make any necessary introductions for anyone who missed the first session. Then have everyone check in by answering one or both of the following questions:

- Growing up, were you more of a "giver" or a "taker" when it came to Christmas holidays and family birthdays? Were you more excited about what you would get, as many children are, or did you enjoy surprising others with gifts?

- When was the last time you gave generously without anyone knowing about it? (It's okay; you can talk about it now.) What prompted you to give so generously then?

HEARING THE WORD

Have someone read aloud the following passage that describes one of the greatest examples of Jesus giving more than he took.

Jesus knew that the Father had put all things under his power, and that he had come from God and was returning to God; so he got up from the meal, took off his outer clothing, and wrapped a towel around his waist. After that, he poured water into a basin and began to wash his disciples' feet, drying them with the towel that was wrapped around him.

When he had finished washing their feet, he put on his clothes and returned to his place. "Do you understand what I have done for you?" he asked them. "You call me 'Teacher' and 'Lord,' and rightly so, for that is what I am. Now that I, your Lord and Teacher, have washed your feet, you also should wash one another's feet.I have set you an example that you should do as I have done for you.Very truly I tell you, no servant is greater than his master, nor is a messenger greater than the one who sent him. Now that you know these things, you will be blessed if you do them.
John 13:3–5, 12–17

Turn to the person next to you, preferably not the same person as last time, and share your answers to the following questions:

- Why is it significant that Jesus "knew that the Father had put all things under his power, and that he had come from God and was returning to God" immediately prior to washing his disciples' feet?

```



```

- What explanation does Jesus offer for choosing to wash the feet of his followers? Why do you suppose Jesus chose to do this on the night before his death?

```



```

TAKING THE HIGH ROAD

Play the video segment for session 2. Use the space on the next page to jot down the big ideas that stand out to you. Then take a few minutes with your group members to discuss what you just watched and explore these concepts in Scripture.

- What surprises you most about Jesus' example here of giving more than he took? Why is his choice to model high-road leadership more impactful than just telling his disciples to serve one another?

```



```

- What is the cost of giving more than you take as a high-road leader? Why is humility an essential element in the example Jesus set for us?

```



```

NOTES

- Peter at first refused Jesus' gift and then asked to have his entire body, not just his feet, washed (John 13:6–11). When has it been challenging for you to accept the gifts offered to you by other high-road leaders? What made it difficult to receive what they offered?

- What barriers, both internal and external, make it difficult for you to give more than you take? How are you overcoming them?

- What are some ways you can set an example for those you lead through a surprising act of service? What's required in order for you to serve them as Jesus served his disciples?

LEADING LIKE JESUS

As this session winds down, complete the following short activity on your own.

- Briefly review the video teaching notes you took or comments you made. Reflect for a moment on the group discussion you just had. Write down any questions you want to answer or thoughts you want to explore further. Underline or circle anything you want to make sure you remember and reflect on prior to your next group session.

In the space below, complete the following sentences as you consider what you will take away from this session—including the teaching, activities, and discussions.

What stands out most to me from this session is...

One way I can follow the example of Jesus and give more than I take is by...

CLOSING IN PRAYER

Go around the group and share any personal prayer requests you would like others to pray about, and then pray for those requests together, either silently or out loud or both. Thank God for setting the ultimate example of generosity by sending his son, Jesus. Ask him to empower you to follow Christ's example and be a high-road leader who gives more than you take.

BEFORE NEXT TIME

Before your group's next meeting, read Chapter 4, "Jesus Didn't Keep Score," in Jesus the High Road Leader, and consider what's required in order for you to avoid keeping score in your relationships.

BETWEEN-SESSIONS PERSONAL STUDY

Similar to the reflective activities after the first session, the exercises below provide opportunities for further application of this week's lesson. Remember, these aren't intended to be homework or another obligation in your busy week. Instead, use them as a way to reflect on the material you've covered and how they can help you be a high-road leader who follows Christ's example. Space is provided below for your answers, or you can use the journal or notebook you started last time.

CHOOSING THE HIGH ROAD

Giving more than you take as a high-road leader requires making sacrifices, sometimes large and sometimes small. We see the ultimate sacrifice made when God sent his only Son, Jesus, to be born in a manger as an infant, to grow and live as a man for more than three decades, and to suffer and die on a cross for our sins. Such a sacrifice could only be the result of our Father's great unconditional love for us, his children: "For God so loved the world that he gave his one and only Son" (John 3:16, emphasis added).

Jesus accepted his Father's will and willingly sacrificed his life on earth to serve those around him. He constantly gave to everyone he encountered through his attitude, words, and actions. Whether healing the sick and infirm, teaching about the radical grace of God, or feeding thousands of hungry people, Jesus did nothing to gratify his ego or pride.

His example calls us to get past our own self-interests and lead with humility. In fact, those who serve their own agendas and promote themselves take the low road and lose sight of their divine purpose, while those willing to give more than they take will be given more responsibility. Jesus explained, "So the last will be first, and the first will be last" (Matt. 20:16). God's Word expresses this clearly as well: "Do nothing out of selfish ambition or vain conceit. Rather, in humility value others above yourselves, not looking to your own interests but each of you to the interests of others" (Phil. 2:3–4).

We find similar instruction emphasized by the apostle Paul, urging us to follow the example of Jesus: "It is more blessed to give than to receive" (Acts 20:35). Translated from the Greek word makarios, "blessed" here literally means "happy in the soul." When we give as high-road leaders like Jesus, we experience the joy of fulfilling our purpose. We give away what God has entrusted to us in order to bless others and advance God's kingdom.

Rather than cling to earthly power and possessions, which becomes an endless cycle of enough never being enough, we can invest in an eternal legacy. Because something good gets released when we willingly give more than we take, we escape the misery that comes from being a miser and discover the joy that comes from being a generous servant-leader. "You'll not likely go wrong here if you keep remembering that our Master said, 'You're far happier giving than getting'" (Acts 20:35, MSG).

Jesus tells us, and shows us through his example, that the value of your life doesn't result from how much you earn or achieve but by how much you give away:

"Do not store up for yourselves treasures on earth, where moths and vermin destroy, and where thieves break in and steal. But store up for yourselves treasures in heaven, where moths and vermin do not destroy, and where thieves do not break in and steal. For where your treasure is, there your heart will be also.
Matthew 6:19–21

Not only does this kind of faithful generosity store up treasures in heaven, but it also opens our hearts to the full abundance of our blessings here on earth. Paul wrote, "Command them to do good, to be rich in good deeds, and to be generous and willing to share. In this way they will lay up treasure for themselves as a firm foundation for the coming age, so that they may take hold of the life that is truly life" (1 Tim. 6:18–19).

- When have you been aware of sacrificing something in order to give more to others? What did it cost you?

- What blessings, or "happiness in your soul," have you experienced as a result of giving more than you take in the way you lead and serve others? What impact has this had on your leadership style?

- If you asked the people you lead and serve where your treasure is being stored, what would they say? How are you creating an eternal legacy by investing in these people?

- When have you struggled to give more than you take in a position of leadership? What might trigger this desire to hold onto more than you give away?

- How are you mentoring others in order to store up heavenly treasure and create a "firm foundation for the coming age"? How does your example reflect the way Jesus gave more than he took?

LEADING BY GOD'S WORD

Throughout God's Word, we are instructed to be givers. We return a portion of our first fruits—our time, talents, and treasure—to him and offer more as we grow in generosity. When we give with an open and generous heart, we reflect the limitless generosity of a good God who delights in giving his children all they need. We can never out give our loving Father, but as we become high-road leaders like his Son, Jesus, we discover the joy that comes from giving sacrificially.

The goal of the enemy, however, is all about taking. Jesus made this contrast clear: "The thief comes only to steal and kill and destroy; I have come that they may have life, and have it to the full" (John 10:10). Rather than giving more than he takes, the devil "prowls around like a roaring lion looking for someone to devour" (1 Peter 5:8). Givers delight in blessing others while takers focus only on what's in it for them. Giving requires humility and faith in God's goodness, while selfishly taking is fueled by fear, insecurity, and a refusal to trust the Lord.

While this contrast is often clear, our motives and judgment can be clouded by circumstances. We see this emerge in an incident in which a very expensive gift was offered to Jesus. He was dining at someone's home when a woman with a reputation for being a sinner crashed the dinner party. She poured rare, expensive perfume on Jesus' feet, weeping and washing them with her tears before drying them with her hair. Her bold offering shocked onlookers with its extravagance and intimacy but illustrates how we are called to give more than we take.

When one of the Pharisees invited Jesus to have dinner with him, he went to the Pharisee's house and reclined at the table. A woman in that town who lived a sinful life learned that Jesus was eating at the Pharisee's house, so she came there with an alabaster jar of perfume. As she stood behind him at his feet weeping, she began to wet his feet with her tears. Then she wiped them with her hair, kissed them and poured perfume on them.

When the Pharisee who had invited him saw this, he said to himself, "If this man were a prophet, he would know who is touching him and what kind of woman she is—that she is a sinner."
Jesus answered him, "Simon, I have something to tell you."

"Tell me, teacher," he said.

"Two people owed money to a certain moneylender. One owed him five hundred denarii, and the other fifty. Neither of them had the money to pay him back, so he forgave the debts of both. Now which of them will love him more?"

Simon replied, "I suppose the one who had the bigger debt forgiven."

"You have judged correctly," Jesus said.

Then he turned toward the woman and said to Simon, "Do you see this woman? I came into your house. You did not give me any water for my feet, but she wet my feet with her tears and wiped them with her hair. You did not give me a kiss, but this woman, from the time I entered, has not stopped kissing my feet. You did not put oil on my head, but she has poured perfume on my feet. Therefore, I tell you, her many sins have been forgiven—as her great love has shown. But whoever has been forgiven little loves little."

Then Jesus said to her, "Your sins are forgiven."

The other guests began to say among themselves, "Who is this who even forgives sins?"
Jesus said to the woman, "Your faith has saved you; go in peace."
Luke 7:36–50

Here we see that our willingness to give more than we take relies on our awareness of God's love and grace. The host, a Pharisee named Simon, criticized the woman, her gift, and Jesus all in one fell swoop. Surely if Jesus was indeed who he claimed to be, then he would rebuke this woman. Instead, Jesus used the situation to reveal how love and forgiveness compels us to give freely.

- How consistently do you give your "first fruits" back to God? How has this impacted your ability to give more than you take as a high-road leader?

- When has the enemy tried to rob you of the joy of being a giver? How have you learned to handle his assaults?

- What stands out or resonates with you in the scene with this woman washing Jesus' feet at the home of the Pharisee? How does this speak to your experience with giving more than you take?

- How does your awareness and gratitude for God's love and grace motivate you to give generously? Do you agree that "whoever has been forgiven little loves little"?

- When was the last time you gave an extravagant gift to someone in order to express your love, appreciation, or gratitude to them? Who would you like to bless with this kind of gift right now?

Taking the High Road

If you want to be a high-road leader like Jesus, you follow his example of giving more than you take without expecting anything in return. He reminds us that giving more than you take begins with an attitude of generosity as your foundation, not a future goal. With open hands and open heart, you cultivate generosity by becoming a conduit for blessing others.

You might be tempted to make your generosity conditional by thinking, "If I won the lottery or inherited a windfall, then I could afford to be generous and help others." You might assume that some day after you retire, then you can afford to volunteer and give your time generously. Jesus, however, makes it clear that high-road leaders give more than they take and start with what they have—not what they might have in the future.

With a generous attitude, you realize that giving is not about the charitable donations you make or the amount of money you contribute. On a daily basis, you can give your attention, your energy, your compassion, and your wisdom to those around you. You can focus on investing in eternal treasures rather than temporary possessions by pouring into the lives of those around you.

Even the smallest act of kindness can have a huge impact on someone else. Jesus said, "And if anyone gives even a cup of cold water to one of these little ones because he is my disciple, I tell you the truth, he will certainly not lose his reward" (Matt. 10:42). High-road leaders know that small acts of giving often produce incredible dividends. They know that texts, emails, and phone calls can encourage and bless others. They know that going above and beyond sets an example for everyone they're leading.

Jesus not only demonstrated this quality but also instructed on this principle in his teaching. Instructing the crowds in what we now call the Sermon on the Mount, he emphasized the importance of not only giving more than you take but of giving more than others expect:

"You have heard that it was said, 'Eye for eye, and tooth for tooth.' But I tell you, do not resist an evil person. If anyone slaps you on the right cheek, turn to them the other cheek also. And if anyone wants to sue you and take your shirt, hand over your coat as well. If anyone forces you to go one mile, go with them two miles. Give to the one who asks you, and do not turn away from the one who wants to borrow from you."
Matthew 5:38–42

Referencing the Old Testament law of "eye for eye, and tooth for tooth," Jesus turned our human understanding of fairness upside down by urging us to do what is probably counterintuitive for many people. He challenged us to do more than is required in situations where most people probably want to do the least. Jesus told us to surprise others by the ways we give more than we take—with no strings attached.

Regardless of how others treat us, Jesus said to overwhelm them with generosity, to surprise them by giving more than they requested. If they demand your shirt, give them your shirt and your coat too. If someone forces you to walk a mile and carry a heavy pack and armor the way Roman soldiers often conscripted citizens to do, then carry their burden not just one mile but two.

This kind of service reflects the way Jesus gave selflessly and commands the attention of those we serve. High-road leaders attract attention because they go beyond what's required of them. They don't stand out when they do the bare minimum—or what they're entitled to do. They stand out because they give more than is reasonably expected. Jesus didn't say that the one who punches the best or hits the hardest wins the fight. No, he said—turn the other cheek.

You cause others to notice when you turn the other cheek or go the second mile. Jesus asks you to give more than what's expected. He didn't ask you to treat others fairly. No, Jesus told us to take the high road and give more, love more and do more than anyone would ever expect. Why? Because our actions say, "There's no good reason to go this second mile except for how it reflects God's goodness and generosity. When I go the second mile, you are going to see Jesus in me." The second mile is where others feel it, not just see it.

As the ultimate high-road leader, Jesus went far beyond the second mile or any human measure in what he gave us. Jesus gave his life so that everyone could be restored to relationship with his Father. He not only told his followers, "Greater love has no one than this: to lay down one's life for one's friends" (John 15:13)—he actually did it. He demonstrated his love by laying down his life for all people. He set the example of being a high-road leader who gives more than he takes.

- What are some ways you can express an attitude of generosity to those you lead and serve? How do they know that you're willing to give more than you take?

- What are some ways you can express an attitude of generosity to those you lead and serve? How do they know that you're willing to give more than you take?

- Who is someone you can surprise this week by going an extra mile and giving more than they expect you to give? Write their name below and then describe when and how you will exceed their expectations by following the instruction Jesus has given.

- How are you laying down your life in order to give more than you take to those you encounter? What have you been unwilling to sacrifice but are now willing to surrender?

66 THE VALUE OF YOUR LIFE ISN'T
DETERMINED BY HOW MUCH YOU ACHIEVE
OR ACCUMULATE BUT BY HOW MUCH OF
YOUR LIFE YOU GIVE AWAY.

JESUS THE HIGH ROAD LEADER, PAGE 45

SESSION 3
JESUS DIDN'T KEEP SCORE

Jesus didn't keep score because he saw a bigger picture. He took a different path, the same one we are encouraged to take as we run the race of our lives.

Jesus the High Road Leader, page 65

GETTING STARTED

Much of life appears to be about keeping score, working to get ahead, pushing to advance yourself beyond those around you. If you're a competitive person, you might enjoy comparing yourself to others and looking for attributes that you believe make you superior to them. Or you may not like comparing and competing but feel resigned to "play the game" in order to prevent others from taking advantage of you. You might feel pressured to perform at work, appear successful, and make sure others view you as a winner.

Scorekeeping, however, always leaves you with a loss. Enough is never enough as you try to win at all costs. You will always make mistakes. You will always find someone who appears happier, wealthier, smarter, more attractive, and more accomplished. Bouncing between feeling one-up or one-down from everyone leaves no room to be who God made you to be.

Jesus shows us through his example that high-road leaders refuse to keep score.

People who follow the low road or settle for the middle road seem to compare, compete, and keep score with anyone and everyone. They strive to get ahead and work to better their image, ego, and achievements. They don't mind using others to advance themselves and their agendas and assume they must promote their own self-interests at all costs.

Jesus, however, always took the high road, and he makes it clear that scorekeeping has no place in our relationships with others. It's worth noting, too, that if anyone had the right to keep score, it was indeed Jesus, God's Son in human flesh, the only perfect man who never sinned. Even though Jesus was first (Col. 1:14–16), he humbled himself and never used his power to place himself first and make others feel inferior. Instead, he served people to show them how much he loved them. Rather than counting who owed him and who deserved a grudge, Jesus used a different kind of math, one based on God's grace, mercy, and forgiveness—all rooted in his unconditional love.

Regardless of how many offenses we've racked up or the negative imbalance of our selfish motives, when we ask Jesus to forgive us, he wipes our slate clean. We are not subject to the score we deserve but instead experience his radical love. Jesus has always loved without conditions, given without expectations, and forgiven without reservations.

To be like Jesus, we must share his desire to love others and forgive them because everyone needs to be forgiven. We must relinquish scorekeeping and practice forgiveness and acceptance on a daily basis. When we love and accept others as human beings in need of God's grace, we show them how Jesus has forgiven us and transformed our lives.

CHECKING IN

Go around the group and check in by answering one or both of the following questions:

- Do you consider yourself a competitive person? What game or sport is one of your favorites in which you compete?

- How often are you aware of "keeping score" with family and friends? What does this look like in your relationships?

HEARING THE WORD

Have someone read aloud the following passage in which even the disciples want to keep score.

Then James and John, the sons of Zebedee, came to him. "Teacher," they said, "we want you to do for us whatever we ask."

"What do you want me to do for you?" He asked.

They replied, "Let one of us sit at your right and the other at your left in your glory."

"You don't know what you are asking," Jesus said. "Can you drink the cup I drink or be baptized with the baptism I am baptized with?

"We can," they answered.

Jesus said to them, "You will drink the cup I drink and be baptized with the baptism I am baptized with, but to sit at My right or left is not for Me to grant. These places belong to those for whom they have been prepared."

When the ten heard about this, they became indignant with James and John. Jesus called them together and said, "You know that those who are regarded as rulers of the Gentiles lord it over them, and their high officials exercise authority over them.Not so with you. Instead, whoever wants to become great among you must be your servant, and whoever wants to be first must be slave of all. For even the Son of Man did not come to be served, but to serve, and to give his life as a ransom for many."

Mark 10:35–45

Now, turn to someone near you and share your answers to the following questions:

• Are you surprised by the request that James and John asked Jesus? Why or why not?

• What assumptions were the disciples making that Jesus had to correct?

TAKING THE HIGH ROAD

Play the video segment for session 3. Use the space on the next page to jot down the big ideas that stand out to you. Then take a few minutes with your group members to discuss what you just watched and explore these concepts in Scripture.

• What motivated or inspired James and John to ask Jesus for an elevated position on either side of Jesus in his glory?

39

NOTES

- What are some ways you've observed others keeping score with you and in their other relationships? How would you describe your connection with them?

- When have you found yourself keeping score with others, either feeling indebted to someone or entitled to their favors or both? What challenges did you encounter when you were keeping score?

- How does an attitude of scorekeeping limit one's relationships with others? With those you lead and serve?

- What stands out to you about the way Jesus refused to keep score and instead always chose to love and forgive others, even his enemies and executioners?

LEADING LIKE JESUS

As this session winds down, complete the following short activity on your own.

- Briefly review the video teaching notes you took or the points you wrote down. Considering the group discussion you just had, jot down any questions you want to answer or thoughts you want to explore further. Underline or circle anything you want to make sure you remember and reflect on prior to your next group session.

- In the space below, complete the following sentences as you consider what you will take away from this session—including the teaching, activities, and discussions.

What resonates with me most from this session has to be...

One way I can make sure I'm not keeping score in my relationships is...

CLOSING IN PRAYER

Go around the group and share any personal prayer requests you would like others to pray about, including any updates about previous requests, and then pray together, either silently or out loud or both. Thank God for not keeping score of your offenses and instead wiping the slate clean through the free gift of salvation through Jesus. Ask him to help you love others the same way, without keeping score and instead extending grace.

BEFORE NEXT TIME

Prior to your group's next meeting, read Chapter 5, "Jesus Acknowledged His Humanness," in Jesus the High Road Leader. Begin thinking about what's required in order for you to follow his example while still acknowledging your own humanity.

BETWEEN-SESSIONS PERSONAL STUDY

Take some time to reflect on the material you've covered this week by engaging in any or all of the following between-sessions exercises. You're invited to use these to process what you've been thinking and applying since your last group time. They're not intended to burden you with homework but to explore the material through more personal study. If your time is limited before your next group meeting, read through all the sections and choose one to complete before your group meets. Begin by stilling yourself before God and inviting the Holy Spirit to guide and empower you as you consider how you can quit keeping score and start loving and leading more like Jesus.

CHOOSING THE HIGH ROAD

Our desire as human beings is to keep score. If someone treats you this way, then you will treat them that way. If they hurt you now, you will file it in your memory until you can hurt them back. If they make you feel inferior to them, then you will work harder and show them you're just as good as they are, if not better.

But here's the problem with living this way: Keeping score is like carrying a suitcase around with you—one that gets heavier and heavier. The more you keep score, the heavier it gets. And you take it everywhere you go. You drag it to work with you. You take it to lunch with you. You sleep with it. You feel the weight of it as you brush your teeth, exercise, or spend time with your family. It's tiring. You grow exhausted by trying harder and yet not scoring higher than those around you.

To be a high-road leader, you must tear up the scorecard, as Jesus does.

If you follow Jesus through the gospels, you will find him refusing to keep score and encouraging others to follow his example. While others despised and shunned Matthew, a tax collector they looked down upon, Jesus called him to be one of his disciples (Matt. 9:9). After miraculously restoring the sight of two blind men, Jesus told them not to tell anyone (Matt. 9:30). He didn't condemn the woman caught in adultery, but instead exhorted her to leave her life of sin (John 8:10–11). He emphasized forgiveness over judgment when a sinful woman anointed his feet (Luke 7:36–50). He taught the importance of forgiving others instead of keeping score in the parable of the unmerciful servant (Matt. 18:21–35). Jesus even forgave His executioners (Luke 23:33–34).

While he certainly had every right to keep score as the Son of God made man, Jesus humbly lowered himself to serve others because He saw a bigger picture. By demonstrating love and humility, Jesus showed us how to live without keeping score. In Hebrews, we're told that followers of Christ should be "looking unto Jesus the author and finisher of our faith; who for the joy that was set before him endured the cross, despising the shame, and is set down at the right hand of the throne of God" (Heb. 12:2, KJV).

Instead of keeping score against those crucifying him, against the condemned man beside him, Jesus despised the shame, endured the cross, and forgave our sins—because ultimately we could never do anything to change the score for ourselves.

Rather than dragging the dead weight of scorekeeping, you are invited to follow Jesus: "Take My yoke upon you and learn from Me, for I am gentle and humble in heart, and you will find rest for your souls. For My yoke is easy and My burden is light" (Matt. 11:29–30).

- How does keeping score attempt to protect you from being hurt in relationships? How does scorekeeping dehumanize other people?

- In addition to the examples mentioned above, can you think of other times when Jesus demonstrated that he did not keep score in his interactions with others?

- Do you agree that scorekeeping only weighs you down more the longer you do it? What other challenges and burdens come with keeping score in your relationships?

- When was the last time you wanted to get even with someone for the way they hurt or offended you? What obstacles stood in the way of forgiving them?

- How does shame perpetuate comparing yourself to others and keeping score? What does it mean for you to follow the example of Jesus and "despise the shame" that often accompanies scorekeeping?

LEADING BY GOD'S WORD

Jesus went to great lengths to demonstrate his unwillingness to keep score—especially with those who often struggled to see their own arrogance. Perhaps nothing reveals this more clearly than the relationship Jesus had with Peter, the brash fisherman who assumed his devotion to his master was unshakable. Basically, Peter seemed to think he was better than his fellow disciples, and he didn't hesitate to say so. At their last supper together before he was arrested, Jesus told his followers:

"This very night you will all fall away on account of me, for it is written:

"'I will strike the shepherd, and the sheep of the flock will be scattered.'

But after I have risen, I will go ahead of you into Galilee."

Peter replied, "Even if all fall away on account of you, I never will."

"Truly I tell you," Jesus answered, "this very night, before the rooster crows, you will disown me three times."

But Peter declared, "Even if I have to die with you, I will never disown you." And all the other disciples said the same.

Matthew 26:31–35, emphasis added

It didn't take long, however, for Peter's resolve to disappear. Set aside dying with Jesus—Peter was unable to even stand up for his master or speak on his behalf:

Now Peter was sitting out in the courtyard, and a servant girl came to him. "You also were with Jesus of Galilee," she said.
But he denied it before them all. "I don't know what you're talking about," he said.
Then he went out to the gateway, where another servant girl saw him and said to the people there, "This fellow was with Jesus of Nazareth."
He denied it again, with an oath: "I don't know the man!"
After a little while, those standing there went up to Peter and said, "Surely you are one of them; your accent gives you away."
Then he began to call down curses, and he swore to them, "I don't know the man!"
Immediately a rooster crowed. Then Peter remembered the word Jesus had spoken: "Before the rooster crows, you will disown me three times." And he went outside and wept bitterly.
Matthew 26:69–75, emphasis added

Even after being informed by Jesus how he would behave and vowing never to disown his Lord, Peter struck out. He crumbled under pressure and lost the only game he claimed mattered to him. Perhaps that's why he wept so bitterly. Peter had failed the person he loved the most.

- If you had been betrayed by Peter like this, how would you have responded?
  What thoughts and feelings would likely rise up in you?

- When has someone you trusted disappointed or betrayed your confidence in them?
  How did you respond in the midst of their failure?

- What stands out most to you in the way Peter claims he would never abandon Jesus? How does Peter's pride blind him to the way scorekeeping is part of his worldview?

- When those you lead and serve fail to live up to your expectations, how do you respond? What does it look like for you to love them the way Jesus went on to love Peter?

- When have you been in Peter's shoes and said or done something you had vowed never to do? How did your failure hurt those you love most?

WALKING THE HIGH ROAD

Peter's story didn't end there, of course. Despite striking out in dramatic fashion by denying he even knew Jesus, Peter did not lose the game—because God does not keep score! Peter was still a disciple, and Jesus still loved him and had a plan for him. This became crystal clear to Peter shortly after the resurrection, when Jesus showed up one morning on the shore to prepare breakfast for him, James, John, and four other disciples who had been fishing (John 21:1–14).

After they finished eating, Jesus made it clear that he loved and forgave him—and wanted Peter to be foundational to spreading the gospel message (John 21:15-19). If Peter was able to come back from failure with Jesus' blessing and fulfill his purpose, then you can too. And you can help and encourage others to do the same—if you stop keeping score.

How can you become more like Jesus and stop keeping score with others? You can start by forgiving others—because everyone needs to be forgiven. Speaking through the prophet Jeremiah, God promised, "I will forgive their wickedness and will remember their sins no more" (Jer. 31:34). He forgives the nightmares of our past so we can reclaim our dreams of the future. To be like Jesus and the Father, we must also practice forgiveness.

To be like Jesus, we must share his desire to love others and forgive them because everyone needs to be forgiven. When Paul described love in his first letter to the Corinthians, he wrote, "Love is patient, love is kind. It does not envy, it does not boast, it is not proud. It does not dishonor others, it is not self-seeking, it is not easily angered, it keeps no record of wrongs" (1 Cor. 13:4–5). Keeping no record of wrongs is simply another way of saying don't keep score. Forgiveness is not about keeping score; it is about losing count.

Perhaps the best way to resist keeping score is to intentionally serve other people. Jesus modeled this in everything he did, but it was never more explicit than on the last night he spent with his disciples when he humbled himself to wash their feet (John 13:3–9). As you explored in the previous session, Jesus was always willing to give more than he took. Such selflessness is only possible when you refuse to keep score.

When we learn to serve others the way Jesus did, we become more confident in who we are and stop comparing ourselves to others. Instead of keeping score, we keep track—but of what we give because, like Jesus, we want to leave more than we take. Consider the difference between keeping score and keeping track:

Keeping Score	Keeping Track
Asks, "Am I getting a return from others?"	Asks "Am I giving a return to others?"
Is Transactional	Is Transformational
Feeds on Competition	Feeds on Consideration
Waits to Be Served by Others	Readily Serves Others

To be a high-road leader like Jesus, you must be willing to serve without keeping score. You keep track of your investment in eternal things rather than keep score over temporary ups and downs. Jesus showed us how to go beyond keeping score by loving without measure.

- How does the way Jesus forgave and loved Peter make it clear that keeping score was not a consideration? What do you suppose Peter ultimately learned from his painful denial of Jesus that night when Christ was arrested?

- When has someone forgiven you, much to your surprise? How did their forgiveness force you to rethink your relationship with them?

- Look through the two lists above that compare "Keeping Score" with "Keeping Track." What stands out personally for you in their distinct contrast?

- Who is someone you need to forgive in order to quit keeping score in your relationship? When can you meet with them to discuss forgiveness and repair this rupture?

JESUS DIDN'T KEEP SCORE BECAUSE HE SAW
A BIGGER PICTURE. HE TOOK A DIFFERENT
PATH, THE SAME ONE WE ARE
ENCOURAGED TO TAKE AS WE RUN THE
RACE OF OUR LIVES.

JESUS THE HIGH ROAD LEADER, PAGE 65

SESSION 4
JESUS ACKNOWLEDGED HIS HUMANNESS

To be a high-road leader like Jesus, we must learn to drop our fear-based façade and stand in sincerity.
Jesus the High Road Leader, page 88

GETTING STARTED

High-road leaders are authentic. Their vulnerability draws others to them because they're willing to risk showing who they really are. They don't pretend to be one thing with some people and then switch masks to act like someone else with others. High-road leaders don't hide behind cultivated reputations or curated images. Their sincerity invites others to know them as they truly are and in turn to be just as authentic.

No one modeled this kind of openness and vulnerability better than Jesus. He acknowledged his humanness as the Son of God through his willingness to be born as a helpless infant in a dirty stable. As Immanuel, God with us in the flesh, Jesus experienced the fullness of the human experience without sinning. He knew the full range of what it means to live in a mortal body, to be hungry and thirsty, to be tired and weary, to be kind and compassionate, to be angry and frustrated, to be sad and lonely.

As the ultimate high-road leader, Jesus never hid his humanness or viewed his mortality as weakness. He let others see his grief as he wept over the loss of his dear friend Lazarus (John 11:33–35), his joy amongst little children (Matt. 19:14), and his longing for the support of his disciples the night before he died (Matt. 26:40–45). Jesus knew that rather than diminishing his deity, acknowledging his humanness helped others experience his love, acceptance, and forgiveness.

For people used to living by the law and viewing God as invisible, such radical accessibility showed the Father's love through the Son's humility to be human. Rather than feeling condemned, ashamed, and unlovable, people realized the extent of God's love in the flesh. Jesus displayed credibility and authority through his divine power to heal, teach, forgive, and perform miracles as well as through his sympathy and understanding of the human condition. "For we do not have a high priest who is unable to empathize with our weaknesses, but we have one who has been tempted in every way, just as we are—yet he did not sin" (Heb. 4:15).

51

If you want to follow the example of Jesus as a high-road leader, then you must acknowledge your humanness as well.

CHECKING IN

Go around the group and check in by answering one of the following questions:

- What three words best describe how you acknowledge your humanness? Do you tend to be "what you see is what you get," or are you more likely to blend in as a chameleon?

```
┌─────────────────────────────────────────────────┐
│                                                 │
│                                                 │
│                                                 │
│                                                 │
│                                                 │
└─────────────────────────────────────────────────┘
```

- What did you learn growing up about the risks involved in letting others see your humanness? What has influenced your willingness to risk vulnerability with those you lead and serve?

```
┌─────────────────────────────────────────────────┐
│                                                 │
│                                                 │
│                                                 │
│                                                 │
│                                                 │
└─────────────────────────────────────────────────┘
```

HEARING THE WORD

Have someone read aloud the following passage showing the challenges Jesus faced as both God and man.

Then Jesus entered a house, and again a crowd gathered, so that he and his disciples were not even able to eat. When his family heard about this, they went to take charge of him, for they said, "He is out of his mind."

And the teachers of the law who came down from Jerusalem said, "He is possessed by Beelzebul! By the prince of demons he is driving out demons."

So Jesus called them over to him and began to speak to them in parables: "How can Satan drive out Satan? If a kingdom is divided against itself, that kingdom cannot stand. If a house is divided against itself, that house cannot stand. And if Satan opposes himself and is divided, he cannot stand; his end has come.In fact, no one can enter a strong man's house without first tying him up. Then he can plunder the strong man's house. Truly I tell you, people can be forgiven all their sins and every slander they utter, but whoever blasphemes against the Holy Spirit will never be forgiven; they are guilty of an eternal sin."

He said this because they were saying, "He has an impure spirit."

Then Jesus' mother and brothers arrived. Standing outside, they sent someone in to call him. A crowd was sitting around him, and they told him, "Your mother and brothers are outside looking for you."

"Who are my mother and my brothers?" He asked.

Then He looked at those seated in a circle around him and said, "Here are My mother and My brothers! Whoever does God's will is My brother and sister and mother."
Mark 3:20–35

Now turn to the person next to you and share your answers to the following questions:

- Why do you suppose even Jesus' family seemed to struggle with recognizing him as the Messiah, the Son of God?

- How does Jesus redefine the meaning of family at the end of this scene?
  What are the implications for those who follow Jesus as a high-road leader?

TAKING THE HIGH ROAD

Play the video segment for session 4. Using the space on the next page, jot down the main points that stand out to you. Then take a few minutes with your group members to discuss what you just watched and explore these concepts in Scripture.

- Of the various ways Jesus acknowledged his humanness, which ones stand out to you? What is it about these that resonates with you?

- Why did so many people struggle with the reality of God in the flesh, Immanuel, in the person of Jesus of Nazareth? How do people continue to struggle with this reality today?

- Why was it essential for Jesus to experience all aspects of being human without giving in to temptation and sinning? How does his humanness affect how you view him?

- What challenges did Jesus face because of his willingness to show his humanness? Make a brief list of the different responses you see in the various people with whom Jesus interacted.

- What has prevented you from acknowledging your humanness to those you lead and serve in the past? What changes have you made in order to be more authentic?

NOTES

LEADING LIKE JESUS

As this session winds down, complete the following short activity on your own.

- Briefly review the notes you took or comments you made during the video teaching. Reflect on the group discussion you just had and write down any questions or thoughts you want to pursue or explore further. Underline or circle anything you want to make sure you remember and reflect on prior to your next group session.

In the space below, complete the following sentences as you consider what you will take away from this session—including the teaching, activities, and discussions.

- As I consider the way Jesus acknowledged his humanness, I am really struck by...

- One way I want to follow the example of Jesus and acknowledge my humanness with those I lead and serve is...

CLOSING IN PRAYER

Go around the group and share any personal prayer requests you would like others to lift up, and then pray for those requests together, either silently or out loud or both. Continue to thank God for your group and all you're learning together about how to be a high-road leader like Jesus. Ask the Holy Spirit to help you see ways you can be more authentic and vulnerable with those you serve.

BEFORE NEXT TIME

- Before your group's next meeting, make sure you have read Chapter 6, "Jesus Did the Right Things for the Right Reasons," in Jesus the High Road Leader. Begin thinking about what's required for you to do the right things for the right reasons.

BETWEEN-SESSIONS
PERSONAL STUDY

By now you know that these questions and exercises are designed to help you go deeper with the material you've been covering and apply it more personally in your life. As you become more intentional about becoming a high-road leader like Jesus, you are likely recognizing changes you want to make in how you relate, lead, and serve. Remember that as you continue following him and practicing principles from his example, you are being transformed into being more like Jesus. Your goal is progress, not perfection.

CHOOSING THE HIGH ROAD

Most of us learn at an early age to seek the approval of others by wearing masks and performing. You may have wanted to fit in so badly that you were willing to sacrifice being authentic in order to conform to the group. If you didn't receive affirmation and learn your God-given worth while growing up, you may rely on pleasing others for your sense of identity and confidence.

Left unchecked, you may lose sight of who you are in Christ and who God has created you to be. Because when you elevate the opinions of others above what God thinks of you, problems are sure to arise. Proverbs explains, "Fear of man will prove to be a snare, but whoever trusts in the LORD is kept safe" (Prov. 29:25). Hiding your weaknesses from other people may feel safe, but it also creates distance as you keep them at arm's length. Your desire for others' approval can also make you defensive and eager to have them see you in ways they will accept and seem to like.

Ultimately, these strategies usually destroy relationships and undermine your ability to serve as a high-road leader like Jesus. Following his example, you must learn to drop your fear-based façade and risk sincerity. Indeed, the very origin of the word "sincerity" illustrates this point. In ancient times, Greek artisans were known to make some of the finest pottery because it rarely cracked. Roman pottery, however, would often crack and need to be covered up and sealed with wax. Out of this practice came a familiar word highlighting the difference between the two kinds of pottery—the word sincere, meaning "without wax."

Sincere means not only solid and genuine but without hiding flaws and covering up imperfections, without glossing over cracks and rough edges. We see this referenced by the apostle Paul, who wrote, "We refuse to wear masks and play games.... Rather, we keep everything we do and say out in the open, the whole truth on display, so that those who want to can see" (2 Cor. 4:2, MSG).

The courage to live authentically comes from trusting God and following Jesus. He knows exactly what you're feeling and experiencing amidst life's ups and downs. He went from being welcomed into Jerusalem with palm branches and hallelujahs to being condemned and executed as a common criminal. He was beloved by many followers but betrayed by one closest to him, Judas. On the night Jesus was arrested, another disciple who had vowed his loyalty, Peter, denied even knowing him at all. Others blasphemed and taunted him, mocking him for telling the truth. Jesus experienced life and death fully as a human being—but through the power of God's Spirit, he rose again on the third day.

Christ's example reminds us to embrace how God has made us and allow his power to work in us as his glory shines through us.

- Growing up, how did you learn to adapt to the expectations of others in order to win their approval? Who influenced the way you learned to please others by concealing your true feelings?

- When have you experienced loss, disappointment, or pain that left you feeling alone and isolated? How does knowing Jesus experienced these same feelings change the way you respond at such times?

- When have you risked being authentic only to feel criticized or punished for it? How have these incidents influenced your willingness to acknowledge your humanness?

- How often do you curate or edit your social media in order to appear a certain way to others? What image are you usually trying to cultivate? Why?

- When have you risked being authentic and been affirmed or validated by others for being so real?

- What other benefits have you experienced from letting others see the "real you"?

LEADING BY GOD'S WORD

Perhaps one of the most powerful examples of Jesus displaying his humanness occurred as he hung on the cross. While experiencing excruciating pain, Jesus made seven statements, which teach us how to take the high road while acknowledging our humanness:

- "Father, forgive them, for they know not what they do" (Luke 23:34, ESV) teaches us to forgive others no matter how brutal the offense.

- "Today you will be with Me in paradise" (Luke 23:43, ESV) teaches us to help others who are experiencing our same struggles.

- "Woman, behold your son!" Then He said to the disciple, "Behold, your mother!" (John 19:26–27, ESV) teaches us to take care of those closest to us.

- "My God, My God, why have You forsaken Me?" (Matt. 27:46, ESV) teaches us to direct our hard questions to God.

- "I thirst!" (John 19:28, ESV) teaches us the importance of acknowledging our needs.

- "It is finished" (John 19:30, ESV) teaches us that in every struggle, there is a purpose and an end.

- "Into your hands I commit My spirit!" (Luke 23:46, ESV) teaches us to trust God.

Notice how basic and real some of these expressions of his humanness are. When Jesus said, "I thirst," he conveyed one of the most fundamental needs of the human body. Amidst his suffering, though, he was also intentional about caring for others, forgiving those who were literally killing him, and calling out to his Father. The full range of his humanness was on display with no attempt to cover up all he thought and felt during these final minutes before death.

If the Son of God acknowledged his humanness during such a bad day, you would be wise to remember that you, too, will have tough times when you can express yourself fully. Times when you must acknowledge your humanness and allow others to help you.

- Which one of Jesus' seven statements stands out or resonates most with you? Why?

- How difficult do you usually find it to express your needs to others? On a scale of 1 to 10, with 1 being "my needs aren't important enough to express" and 10 being "my needs remind me of my humanness," what score reflects the way you handle your needs before others?

- Which of the seven statements Jesus made while dying on the cross surprises you most? Why do you find this statement unexpected or startling?

- Who are the people you rely on most often to help meet your relational and social needs? Your needs for spiritual fellowship and community?

- Which one of your needs are you usually reluctant to express before others? What is it about this need that makes you uncomfortable to share it?

- When have you risked being authentic and been affirmed or validated by others for being so real? What other benefits have you experienced from letting others see the "real you"?

WALKING THE HIGH ROAD

Jesus acknowledged his humanness during a time when life wasn't particularly easy. He was born when his homeland, Israel, had been conquered and occupied by the Roman Empire. Rather than being born into wealth and luxury, Jesus entered this world in human form as a baby with a feeding trough for animals as his bed.

From there, his circumstances didn't improve for quite a while. While barely a toddler, his family had to flee to Egypt for his safety. His earthly father was a tradesman, a carpenter, neither wealthy nor powerful. After beginning his public ministry, Jesus experienced skepticism and even ridicule from those who knew him growing up, including family members. Many people scoffed at the idea that someone from "the other side of the tracks" could be the Son of God.

But this is precisely why Jesus came to earth in human form—to experience all of life, including its many hardships, prejudices, and challenges. God's Word explains, "That's why he had to enter into every detail of human life. Then, when he came before God as high priest to get rid of the people's sins, he would have already experienced it all himself—all the pain, all the testing—and would be able to help where help was needed" (Heb. 2:17–18 MSG, emphasis added). Jesus, our High Priest and ultimate high-road leader, knows the full extent of what it meant to be human while able to go before God the Father to expiate our sins.

While you may be tempted to imagine Jesus in a flowing robe happily traipsing from place to place healing the sick, forgiving sinners, and welcoming outcasts, such an idyllic vision misses so much of how Jesus acknowledged his humanness. You must remember that prior to entering public ministry and leading disciples for three years, Jesus had spent most of his life doing manual labor as a carpenter, the trade he learned from his earthly father, Joseph.

Jesus' humble background may have caught some people by surprise even as it helped many others relate to him. But his example makes it clear that God does not focus on earthly qualifications and abilities. Through his humility, compassion, and authenticity, Jesus attracted others because he acknowledged his humanness and willingly served his Father by sacrificing himself. Similarly, high-road leaders endear themselves to others when they don't see themselves as self-qualified or world-qualified—but God-qualified.

- What qualifications come to mind when you consider your present responsibilities and roles? Which ones are based on earthly criteria, and which are the result of being called and equipped by God?

- Which personal events, experiences, and circumstances have uniquely qualified you to connect with others you now serve? How has God used your life experiences—particularly the hardships and challenges—to equip you to lead?

- How do you usually respond to critics and detractors who want to focus on the qualifications you lack for your current position? What aspects of your character and qualifications do they overlook by focusing on their own standards rather than God's?

- What's one area of your leadership where you can risk more vulnerability and authenticity? How might others respond if they knew more of your sincerity?

To be a high-road leader like Jesus, we must learn to drop our fear-based façade and stand in sincerity.

JESUS THE HIGH ROAD LEADER, PAGE 88

SESSION 5
Jesus Did the Right Things For the Right Reasons

Our motives are wrong when we are number one on our agenda. With our focus on God, our motives become purified.

Jesus the High Road Leader, page 105

Getting Started

The way you lead and serve depends on your motives. When you lead others only for your own benefit, you're manipulating them to promote yourself and your agenda. Low-road leaders typically operate this way, focusing all their efforts on self-promotion. Middle-road leaders may be motivated by helping others, but only after helping themselves first.

Only high-road leaders intentionally focus on how they can help others and improve our world. They know that when you lead others for their benefit or for mutual advantage, you're motivating others to do the same. High-road leaders are motivated by God's Word and led by the Holy Spirit in order to align with what pleases God instead of people.

This is how Jesus led. As the ultimate high-road leader, he did the right things for the right reasons. Jesus never failed to see his Father's bigger picture and act for the right reasons. He always valued relationships over rules, truth over law, and servanthood over religion. He never allowed legalism to displace love. Over and over, we see him respond to people with love.

Jesus repeatedly demonstrated how love motivated him in his interactions with those around him. When his disciple Peter walked on water and began to sink, Jesus lifted him up rather than rebuking him for lack of faith (Matt. 14:31). When Jesus learned of John the Baptist's death, he withdrew to grieve in private. Nonetheless, when the crowds followed him, Jesus refused to ignore their needs and showed compassion by healing the sick (Matt. 14:13–14). Even though he knew Judas was about to betray him, Jesus washed his feet along with those of the other disciples (John 13:5). When challenged to defend himself before the high priest, Jesus remained silent in order to fulfill his sacrifice by dying on the cross (Matt. 26:62–63).

Repeatedly, Jesus made it clear that his focus was on obeying and pleasing his Father's will regardless of how others responded. His example challenges us to act beyond our own self-interests. If you want to be a high-road leader like Jesus, then your motives must be grounded in doing the right things for the right reasons.

CHECKING IN

Go around the group and check in by answering one of the following questions:

- What challenges arise when relationships are prioritized over rules?

- When have you struggled to do the right thing for the right reason?

HEARING THE WORD

Have someone read aloud the following passage about being motivated to please God rather than to perform for others.

"Be especially careful when you are trying to be good so that you don't make a performance out of it. It might be good theater, but the God who made you won't be applauding.

"When you do something for someone else, don't call attention to yourself. You've seen them in action, I'm sure— 'playactors' I call them—treating prayer meeting and street corner alike as a stage, acting compassionate as long as someone is watching, playing to the crowds. They get applause, true, but that's all they get. When you help someone out, don't think about how it looks. Just do it—quietly and unobtrusively. That is the way your God, who conceived you in love, working behind the scenes, helps you out."

Matthew 6:1–4, MSG

Pair up with someone new and share your answers to the following questions:

- In our social media-saturated culture, what challenges arise when you focus on what God wants regardless of what others may think?

- How do you keep your motives aligned with God rather than focused on how others will perceive what you say and do?

TAKING THE HIGH ROAD

Play the video segment for session 5. Use the space on the next page to note the ideas that stand out to you. Then take a few minutes with your group members to discuss what you just watched and explore these concepts in Scripture.

- When have you witnessed others doing the right things for the wrong reasons? What do you suppose motivated them?

- What are some ways to keep your motives focused on pleasing God rather than performing for the perception of others? Which ways help you the most?

- When have others questioned your motives as you've followed the example of Jesus? How did you respond to them?

- Which encounters of Jesus interacting with others stands out for you? How do they inspire or strengthen your ability to do the right things for the right reasons?

- What current decision, challenge, or conflict are you facing as a servant-leader to others? What passage or scene from Scripture speaks to this situation?

NOTES

LEADING LIKE JESUS

As this session winds down, complete the following short activity on your own.

Take a few moments to review the video teaching notes you took or comments you made. Think about what stands out to you in the group discussion you just had as well. Jot down any questions or thoughts you want to consider or explore further. Underline or circle anything you want to make sure you remember and reflect on prior to your next group session.

In the space below, complete the following sentences as you consider what you will take away from this session—including the teaching, activities, and discussions.

- The takeaway idea from this session that I want to remember and apply is...

- One way I keep my motives focused on pleasing God rather than others is...

CLOSING IN PRAYER

Share any personal prayer requests or updates you would like other group members to pray about, and then pray for those requests together, either silently or out loud or both. Give thanks for all God is revealing to you in this group and the ways you're learning to be more like Jesus as a high-road leader. Ask God to give you strength, wisdom, and courage to always do the right things for the right reasons.

BEFORE NEXT TIME

Before your group meets again, be sure to read Chapter 7, "Jesus Embraced Authenticity," in Jesus the High Road Leader, and start considering what's required in order for you to follow his example and be more authentic in the way you lead.

BETWEEN-SESSIONS PERSONAL STUDY

Use this personal study as a way to continue processing everything you're learning and experiencing, both from the group sessions as well as reading Jesus the High Road Leader. You might also use this time between sessions to begin reflecting on how your understanding of high-road leadership is changing and expanding.

Spend a few minutes in prayer before diving into the questions and exercises below. Ask God to give you wisdom and discernment about what to focus on and how to use everything you're learning. If some questions or sections don't resonate with you right now, feel free to skip over them and seek out the ones that do. Remember, this is not busy work but a way for you to draw closer to God as you go deeper into the material. Naturally, some points will seem more personally relevant than others as the Holy Spirit guides you.

CHOOSING THE HIGH ROAD

Of all the right things high-road leaders do for the right reasons, perhaps none is more important than forgiveness. If you have received God's grace through the sacrifice of Jesus on the cross, then you know how powerful forgiveness can be. It transforms hearts and lives. It is the heart of the gospel message. It is the ultimate right thing for the right reason. Forgiveness reconciles relationships, saves lives, and heals families.

High-road living requires forgiving others—it isn't optional. Jesus emphasized the importance of forgiveness when he included it in his teaching on how we should pray. After praising God, we can ask him to do many things for us: grant us provision, give us protection, and deliver us from evil. But Jesus also includes one thing we must do: forgive others. He said, "Forgive us our debts as we forgive our debtors" (Matt. 6:12). To underline his point, Jesus explained, "For if you forgive other people when they sin against you, your heavenly Father will also forgive you. But if you do not forgive others their sins, your Father will not forgive your sins" (Matt. 6:14–15).

As a high-road leader following the example of Jesus, you know that forgiveness is essential —personally and professionally—to how you serve those around you. This can be challenging when others hurt us with their words or actions.

Yet this is exactly what Jesus asks us to do. He set the standard, and we will also be judged by that standard. Why? Because not only has everyone been offended or injured by others—we have all done our share of hurting others too. Whether intentionally or not, we sin against others and need them to forgive us. If God has forgiven us for everything we've done, then we must extend the same unconditional forgiveness to others.

Do you freely forgive others? Do you really want God to use the way you regard others as the model for how he will forgive you? Remembering how Jesus paid the price for your sins—all of them—can help motivate you to always forgive for the right reason.

When you forgive others and seek their forgiveness for your transgressions, you realize just how powerful forgiveness can be. It not only blesses others, but it also changes your own heart. That's no small task, and it's something rules cannot accomplish. Many people would rather rewrite a law because it's easier than rewriting a heart. But when our hearts change, we become more like Jesus. Only a changed heart will do the right things for the right reasons.

- What role has forgiveness played in how you lead and serve others? How have you demonstrated the importance of forgiveness to those around you?

- When was the last time you extended grace to someone who offended you? When was the last time you apologized and asked someone to forgive you?

- What does it look like for you to "forgive your debtors" as God has forgiven you? How has your relationship with Jesus changed the way you respond to those who hurt you or mean you harm?

- When have you witnessed the power of forgiveness at work in the lives of those you lead and serve? What difference has forgiveness made in how those you lead treat one another?

- Is there someone you need to forgive right now in order to demonstrate how God has forgiven you? Is there someone you need to ask to forgive you?

LEADING BY GOD'S WORD

Doing the right things for the wrong reasons eventually forces you to reexamine your motives. We see a striking example of this in the parable Jesus told about the lost, or prodigal, son. The younger son asked his father for his inheritance and squandered it all on wild living—clearly the wrong thing for the wrong reason.

After hitting rock bottom, however, he repented, humbled himself, and returned home prepared to face the consequences of how he had hurt his father and wasted his inheritance. To his great surprise, the younger son was welcomed home by his father with open arms. The father thought he had lost his son and was so overjoyed to have him home again that he threw a big party. It sounds like a happy ending, only the story doesn't end there.

The prodigal's older brother had a big problem with how their father was handling things. This elder son was doing the right things but with the wrong motives. Here's how Jesus described the problem:

"All this time his older son was out in the field. When the day's work was done he came in. As he approached the house, he heard the music and dancing. Calling over one of the houseboys, he asked what was going on. He told him, 'Your brother came home. Your father has ordered a feast—barbecued beef!—because he has him home safe and sound.'

"The older brother stomped off in an angry sulk and refused to join in. His father came out and tried to talk to him, but he wouldn't listen. The son said, 'Look how many years I've stayed here serving you, never giving you one moment of grief, but have you ever thrown a party for me and my friends? Then this son of yours who has thrown away your money on whores shows up and you go all out with a feast!'

His father said, 'Son, you don't understand. You're with me all the time, and everything that is mine is yours—but this is a wonderful time, and we had to celebrate. This brother of yours was dead, and he's alive! He was lost, and he's found!'" Luke 15:25–32, MSG

While the older brother remained home, worked hard, and lived responsibly, he didn't have the loving heart of his father. His actions were right, but his attitude was wrong. Every day he was close to his father, but he didn't connect with him relationally. He didn't long to see his lost brother return. And he didn't share the joy of his father when his brother did come home. Perhaps the older son thought he had to earn his father's favor because he certainly didn't understand that everything his father had was already his.

If you want to do the right things for the right reasons, then you must guard against becoming like the older brother. Your motives always matter to God. Jesus emphasized God's perspective on this by quoting the prophet Hosea, saying, "I desire mercy, not sacrifice" (Matt. 9:13).
God wants you to love people as he has loved you. Receiving his love motivates you to love them even in their worst moments. Paul reminds us that it doesn't matter how many right things we do if we don't have the right motive. He said we can do great things—speak in tongues, deliver prophecies, exhibit mountain-moving faith, fathom mysteries, possess knowledge, give to the poor, and endure hardship—but if we "do not have love," we "gain nothing" (1 Cor. 13:1–3).

- What do you suppose the older brother had assumed about his relationship with his father?
  What did that son believe to be the basis for his father's love?

- When have you felt overlooked and resentful like the older brother of the prodigal?
  What caused the misalignment between your actions and your motives?

- When someone is doing the right things for the wrong reasons, how can you tell?
  How do their motives tend to surface in such situations based on your experience?

- As you consider the various experiences of your life, who do you identify with most easily in this parable? The father, the younger son, or the older brother? Why?

- What are some ways to guard against becoming bitter, angry, and resentful like the older brother?

WALKING THE HIGH ROAD

If you want to see how Jesus did the right thing for the right reason in a tricky situation, just consider the way he approached the Sabbath. You may recall that Jewish religious laws required everyone at that time to follow strict guidelines about what could and could not be done in order to keep the Sabbath set aside as a holy day of rest. Looking for any reason to criticize Jesus, the Jewish religious leaders called Pharisees were quick to point out times when they believed Jesus violated Sabbath laws:

One Sabbath day he was walking through a field of ripe grain. As his disciples made a path, they pulled off heads of grain. The Pharisees told on them to Jesus: "Look, your disciples are breaking Sabbath rules!"

Jesus said, "Really? Haven't you ever read what David did when he was hungry, along with those who were with him? How he entered the sanctuary and ate fresh bread off the altar, with the Chief Priest Abiathar right there watching—holy bread that no one but priests were allowed to eat—and handed it out to his companions?" Then Jesus said, "The Sabbath was made to serve us; we weren't made to serve the Sabbath." Mark 2:23–27, MSG

We also see Jesus helping and healing broken people on the Sabbath, proof that he loved people, not the man-made rules of the religious leaders.

Then he went back in the meeting place where he found a man with a crippled hand. The Pharisees had their eyes on Jesus to see if he would heal him, hoping to catch him in a Sabbath infraction. He said to the man with the crippled hand, "Stand here where we can see you."

Then he spoke to the people: "What kind of action suits the Sabbath best? Doing good or doing evil? Helping people or leaving them helpless?" No one said a word.

He looked them in the eye, one after another, angry now, furious at their hard-nosed religion. He said to the man, "Hold out your hand." He held it out—it was as good as new! The Pharisees got out as fast as they could, sputtering about how they would join forces with Herod's followers and ruin him. Mark 3:1–6, MSG

When you love people, value them, and want to help them, it's very difficult for your motives to be wrong. Yet as we see with the way the Pharisees confronted Jesus, many people prefer to put rules over relationships. They rely on legalism, policing others to obey rules and regulations to elevate their own authority and validate their own egos. They pretended to be perfect, and instead of loving others, they demanded that others follow rules they couldn't follow themselves.

Jesus didn't hesitate to call out their pretense and hypocrisy: "They tie up heavy, cumbersome loads and put them on other people's shoulders, but they themselves are not willing to lift a finger to move them." He went on to say, "Woe to you, teachers of the law and Pharisees, you hypocrites! You clean the outside of the cup and dish, but inside they are full of greed and self-indulgence" (Matt. 23:4, 25).

Legalism appears to do the right things but not for the right reasons.

Jesus always put people first—not manmade rules and judgments.

- When have you felt challenged to do the right thing for the right reason in a tricky situation? How did you handle the criticism or judgment you received from others?

- What are some rules and social expectations, either unspoken or explicit, that people tend to prioritize over relationships? Which one do you find especially troublesome?

- Why do you suppose Jesus was so direct in his rebuke of the Pharisees and their regard for Sabbath laws? Why do you think their attitudes upset him so much?

- How can you guard against legalism in the way you lead and serve others? What are some signs that you're likely slipping off the high road and losing sight of the right reasons for what you're doing?

" OUR MOTIVES ARE WRONG WHEN WE ARE NUMBER ONE ON OUR AGENDA. WITH OUR FOCUS ON GOD, OUR MOTIVES BECOME PURIFIED.

JESUS THE HIGH ROAD LEADER, PAGE 105

SESSION 6
JESUS EMBRACED AUTHENTICITY

If you desire to lead people, you must be aware of and accept your authentic self
before you can allow others to know who you are and communicate why they
should follow you.

Jesus the High Road Leader, page 126

GETTING STARTED

High-road leaders know that authenticity matters. They practice authenticity by doing what they say they will do and aligning their actions with their words. They demonstrate to those they lead as well as everyone around them that they are the same person regardless of what they're doing and where they are. Authenticity leaves no room for pretense, posturing, or positioning oneself in order to appear a certain way. Embracing authenticity invites others to see who you really are as opposed to a calculated persona, convenient mask, or curated image.

Authenticity draws others to you and garners their respect. Even if they don't agree with you or particularly like you, they will respect you if you are authentic. Your willingness to be real with others welcomes them to be real with you. They realize they can trust you to be who you appear to be, not a chameleon who adapts themselves to please whoever they're around. You will also discover that authenticity frees you to be the same person you are at home as you are at work, the same person in the stands at a ballgame as around the table in the boardroom.

Without authenticity, leaders continually seem to shift and pivot, always trying to read the room or forecast which way the wind will blow. Living and leading inauthentically, however, leaves a glaring gap between what you claim to believe and what you actually demonstrate matters to you through your actions. Others will notice and quickly conclude that you hold them to one standard while typically making yourself the exception.

Jesus embraced authenticity by always practicing what he preached. His authenticity as both God and man revealed his Father's love in action: "The Word [God] became a human being and lived here with us. We saw his true glory, the glory of the only Son of the Father. From him the complete gifts of undeserved grace and truth have come down to us" (John 1:14, CEV). Jesus was the ultimate, real-deal, authentic high-road leader, humbling himself so that he would exalt his heavenly Father and serve those around him. To be more like him, we need to be willing to be our authentic selves.

CHECKING IN

Check in with other group members by having everyone answer one of the following questions:

- How can you tell when someone is being authentically themselves? What clues reveal a person's authenticity?

- Who do you know well that exemplifies authenticity? How would you describe their willingness to let others know who they really are?

HEARING THE WORD

Have someone read aloud the following passage in which Jesus displays authenticity by revealing his relationship with his Father.

"I am the way and the truth and the life. No one comes to the Father except through me. If you really know me, you will know my Father as well. From now on, you do know him and have seen him." Philip said, "Lord, show us the Father and that will be enough for us."

Jesus answered: "Don't you know me, Philip, even after I have been among you such a long time? Anyone who has seen me has seen the Father. How can you say, 'Show us the Father'? Don't you believe that I am in the Father, and that the Father is in me? The words I say to you I do not speak on my own authority. Rather, it is the Father, living in me, who is doing his work. Believe me when I say that I am in the Father and the Father is in me; or at least believe on the evidence of the works themselves. Very truly I tell you, whoever believes in me will do the works I have been doing, and they will do even greater things than these, because I am going to the Father. And I will do whatever you ask in my name, so that the Father may be glorified in the Son. You may ask me for anything in my name, and I will do it.
John 14:6–14

Now turn to someone near you and share your answers to the following questions:

- Why is his relationship with his Father essential to Jesus' authenticity?

- Why do you suppose the disciples struggled with understanding the way Jesus authentically revealed himself here?

TAKING THE HIGH ROAD

Play the video segment for session 6. Use the space on the next page to jot down the big ideas that stand out to you. Then take a few minutes with your group members to discuss what you just watched and explore these concepts in Scripture.

- What are some examples of the way Jesus aligned his actions with his words? How did he demonstrate who he said he was?

- Why do you suppose Jesus was so adamant about exposing the hypocrisy of the Pharisees and Jewish religious leaders? Do you agree that hypocrisy is the opposite of authenticity?

- What cultural and religious expectations caused some people to struggle accepting Jesus when they encountered him? How did his authenticity apparently disappoint them?

NOTES

- What do you risk when you let others see and know you authentically? What benefits have you experienced from being authentic?

- When have you been criticized, shamed, or cancelled for being authentic? How have such incidents affected the way you engage with others?

LEADING LIKE JESUS

As this session winds down, complete the following short activity on your own.

Briefly review any notes you took during the video teaching or group discussion time. Write down any other questions or thoughts you want to remember to explore further. Underline or circle anything that especially resonates with your own experience.

In the space below, complete the following sentences as you consider what you will take away from this session—including the teaching, activities, and discussions.

- What's important for me to remember about authenticity is...

- One way I want to follow the example of Jesus in being authentic is...

CLOSING IN PRAYER

Go around the group and share any personal prayer requests or updates you would like others to pray about, and then lift up those requests together, either silently or out loud or both. Thank Jesus for the way he embraced authenticity during his time on earth and exemplified high-road leadership. Ask the Holy Spirit to empower you as you allow others to know your authentic self.

BEFORE NEXT TIME

Before your group's next meeting, read Chapter 8, "Jesus Placed People above His Agenda," in Jesus the High Road Leader, and consider what's required in order for you to follow his example and focus on relationships and not results.

BETWEEN-SESSIONS
PERSONAL STUDY

Your willingness to live authentically often relies on how secure you feel in your identity as an overcomer and co-heir with Christ. When you remain anchored by who God says you are and what he has uniquely created and equipped you to do, then you can lead and serve without constantly worrying about what others think of you. The questions and exercises below are designed to help you grow in your faith so that you can more fully follow the example of Jesus as a high-road leader. As you've done previously, use the space below to respond and process how this session's big ideas apply to you.

CHOOSING THE HIGH ROAD

Jesus embraced authenticity because he was comfortable with his true identity. He communicated his authentic identity as both God and man in everything he said and did. Throughout the Gospel of John, Jesus defined himself to others using four key "I am" statements that provide insight for us as well. These four statements show us how to embrace authenticity as high-road leaders like Jesus.

"I Am the Bread of Life" (John 6:35).

Jesus offered everyone real fulfillment, saying, "I am the bread of life. Whoever comes to me will never go hungry, and whoever believes in me will never be thirsty" (John 6:35). He knew what he had to offer—that who he was would satisfy and nourish every soul. Similarly, high-road leaders embrace authenticity because they know what they have to offer to others. No matter the setting or circumstances, you should consider how you can satisfy a longing or meet a need for those around you rather than looking to benefit yourself. Because you are nourished by the Bread of Life, you can nourish others through your contribution.

"I Am the Light of the World" (John 8:12).

Jesus made it clear that he came to illuminate the darkness of the world by providing light and life to those who follow him: "I am the light of the world. Whoever follows me will never walk in darkness, but will have the light of life" (John 8:12). Jesus offers real forgiveness with authentic love and grace rather than shame and condemnation: "For God did not send his Son into the world to condemn the world, but to save the world through him" (John 3:17). God loves you just as you are—but too much to leave you that way. And he wants you to share his love with others, to be a light in the world's darkness.

"I Am the Gate" (John 10:9).

By stating, "I am the gate; whoever enters through me will be saved. They will come in and go out, and find pasture" (John 10:9), Jesus revealed a new way of relating to God that people could experience. Drawing on the relationship between sheep and the caring shepherd who tends them, Jesus emphasized the importance of trust. When we recognize the loving power of Jesus and rest in the security of his protection, we can provide access and also protection for those we lead and serve. High-road shepherds open doors and show others the way forward.

"I Am the Resurrection" (John 11:25).

Jesus said, "I am the resurrection and the life. The one who believes in me will live, even though they die; and whoever lives by believing in me will never die. Do you believe this?" (John 11:25–26). His offer goes beyond mortal limits and temporary fixes—Jesus gives us an eternal promise. He anchors us in our identity as a beloved child of God, fearfully and wonderfully made. He empowers us to discover and live out our divine purpose.

To be high-road leaders like Jesus, we should constantly be looking for ways to bring new life to those around us. Like Jesus, we should look for ways to bring every dead end back to life and give others a fresh start. Jesus set the example for us that not even death is final. It's never too late to experience a rebirth, a renewal, a resurrection.

- Which of these four "I am" statements resonates most with you right now? Why do you suppose it stands out?

- Which of the four statements seems most challenging or daunting for you to emulate? Why?

- What high-road leadership qualities are expressed by each of these four declarations of Jesus' identity? Jot them down below:

"I Am the Bread of Life" (John 6:35).

High-road leadership qualities:

"I Am the Light of the World" (John 8:12).

High-road leadership qualities:

"I Am the Gate" (John 10:9).

High-road leadership qualities:

"I Am the Resurrection" (John 11:25).

High-road leadership qualities:

- Which of the four statements seems most challenging or daunting for you to emulate? Why?

- Who are the mentors, peer leaders, and leaders in your life who exemplify these qualities? How have they inspired you to be more like Jesus by embracing authenticity?

- What steps can you take to provide more protection and security for those in your care? How can you demonstrate your authentic desire to accept and nurture them?

LEADING BY GOD'S WORD

We see how Jesus valued authenticity by the way he lived, taught, and stood up for it—and by the way he challenged people to respond to the conviction of authenticity. He had little regard for religious institutional posturing or those who were personally hypocrites. Jesus specifically challenged his followers to focus on their own shortcomings rather than looking to blame or condemn others:

Why do you look at the speck of sawdust in your brother's eye and pay no attention to the plank in your own eye? How can you say to your brother, 'Let me take the speck out of your eye,' when all the time there is a plank in your own eye? You hypocrite, first take the plank out of your own eye, and then you will see clearly to remove the speck from your brother's eye.
Matthew 7:3–5

If you want to lead authentically as a high-road leader, you must focus on the plank in your own eye before calling out the speck of sawdust in someone else's. Humbly and sincerely, you must model an awareness of your weaknesses, flaws, and mistakes, and possess a willingness to seek forgiveness. High-road leaders do not pretend that they have everything together or that they have arrived at perfection. They are real with others about their struggles, challenges, and mistakes.

Self-promoting pretentious leaders, on the other hand, exemplify hypocrisy. We see a sharp contrast between authenticity and hypocrisy in the encounters Jesus had with the Jewish religious leaders. To maintain their status and power, they often laid plans to trap him or bait him to take political positions:

The Pharisees went out and laid plans to trap him in his words. They sent their disciples to him along with the Herodians. "Teacher," they said, "we know that you are a man of integrity and that you teach the way of God in accordance with the truth. You aren't swayed by others, because you pay no attention to who they are. Tell us then, what is your opinion? Is it right to pay the imperial tax to Caesar or not?"

But Jesus, knowing their evil intent, said, "You hypocrites, why are you trying to trap me? Show me the coin used for paying the tax." They brought him a denarius, and he asked them, "Whose image is this? And whose inscription?"

"Caesar's," they replied.

Then he said to them, "So give back to Caesar what is Caesar's, and to God what is God's."
When they heard this, they were amazed. So they left him and went away.
Matthew 22:15–22

86

Jesus always saw through these traps and exposed the questioners' hypocrisy. He called out the Pharisees even more directly in another instance, telling his disciples and the crowd that had gathered, "They tie up heavy, cumbersome loads and put them on other people's shoulders, but they themselves are not willing to lift a finger to move them" (Matt. 23:4). Always setting the example as God with us, Jesus consistently humbled himself, and lead by serving with authenticity.

- How often do you take responsibility for your own shortcomings and mistakes rather than blaming others? How does being authentic and honest about your weaknesses improve your ability to lead?

- When have you had to confront hypocrisy in the midst of your team, organization, church, or institution? How did the way Jesus confronted the Pharisees give you guidance?

- What's one log in your own eye that you're working on removing? How does being humbly aware of this log prevent you from criticizing or blaming others too quickly?

- How have you managed to sidestep the traps that others have set to undermine your authenticity? When have you encountered such a trap most recently?

How does the way Jesus embraced authenticity cause you to rethink others' opinions of you as a leader? What steps have you taken to be more authentically yourself with those you lead and serve?

WALKING THE HIGH ROAD

Authenticity is essential in order for meaningful relationships to grow and thrive. We all long to be known and accepted for who we are. Real life-change happens in the context of relationships where we are free to be our messy, glorious selves—where we know that we are wanted and in turn we want to do life with those in community with us. "So in Christ we, though many, form one body, and each member belongs to all the others" (Rom. 12:5).

Authentic relationships help us know ourselves better, know others better, and know God better. But that doesn't mean they come naturally. No, we have to cultivate them. One tool that many leaders find helpful in thinking through the value of authentic relationships is called the Johari Window. Developed by psychologists Joseph Luft and Harrington Ingham in 1955, this tool helps us understand ourselves, which makes us more authentic. The Johari Window reveals four areas of awareness and can be diagrammed like this:

	Known to Self	Unknown to Self
Known to Others	Arena	Blind Spot
Unknown to Others	Mask	Potential

ARENA

This first quadrant reflects the public you, representing what you and others know about you. If you only prioritize how others see you, then you resort to pretense, posture, and position to shape others' perceptions. To be a high-road leader like Jesus, you must seek God's approval above other people's and allow the arena to reflect an alignment of both your external and internal selves—your authenticity.

MASK

This window represents what we know about ourselves but hide from others—our secrets, hidden thoughts, fears, and some other emotions. We all have areas we want to hide, but we cannot be authentic if we're hiding. People stay as sick as their secrets. To be like Jesus, we must be transparent and vulnerable, removing our masks and risking vulnerability. When we are honest and authentic, we inspire others to let down their masks and be known as well.

BLIND SPOT

The third quadrant indicates areas others can see about you that you cannot see about yourself. You need to do the work to know what you don't know if you hope to be authentic. You need help from others willing to have your back and show you what you do not know or realize about yourself.

For you to develop authenticity in this quadrant, you must be in relationships with people you trust. You need faithful friends who know you and care for you, who are willing to point out your blind spots—not acquaintances, critics, or enemies. Proverbs says, "Faithful are the wounds of a friend, but the kisses of an enemy are deceitful" (Prov. 27:6, NKJV).

POTENTIAL

The fourth quadrant represents what you and others don't know about yourself. It's what only God knows. You have unrealized potential, and you will never reach it alone. You need others to help you discover it, exercise it, and refine it. "As iron sharpens iron, so one person sharpens another" (Prov. 27:17).

In a community of people committed to authenticity, you discover that we is more powerful than me. Collaboration and cooperation with others produce results that are more than the sum of individual contributions. Authentic people in community provide support and encouragement, constructive feedback and helpful strategies, knowing that this is how everyone grows and fulfills their potential.

Embracing authenticity as Jesus modeled it requires us to acknowledge our strengths and our weaknesses, our reliance on God and on other people. When you commit to being authentic, you inherently invest in your integrity. High-road leaders know that embracing authenticity draws them closer to Jesus even as it points others to him as well.

	Known to Self	Unknown to Self
Known to Others	Arena	Blind Spot
Unknown to Others	Mask	Potential

Using the Johari Window diagram above, go through each of the four quadrants and jot down what comes to mind about yourself. Don't worry about complete sentences, spelling, or punctuation. Just write down words and phrases that fit your own awareness of yourself in each window.

- Which of the four quadrants proved the most difficult to discern and express? Why do you suppose this one causes you to struggle?

- Who are the individuals who have your back and help you see your blind spots? How have they helped you become a more authentic leader?

- What measures have you taken to avoid cultivating masks that attempt to manipulate the way others see you? How do you exercise discernment about what and with whom to share your secrets?

" If you desire to lead people, you must be aware of and accept your authentic self before you can allow others to know who you are and communicate why they should follow you.

JESUS THE HIGH ROAD LEADER, PAGE 126

SESSION 7
JESUS PLACED PEOPLE ABOVE HIS AGENDA

When we value people, give them hope, and place them above our agenda, we become most like Jesus.

Jesus the High Road Leader, page 153

GETTING STARTED

Jesus challenged everyone he encountered during his time on earth to reconsider how they interacted with others. He called them, just as he calls us today, to a higher level of living: to put people and relationships ahead of ourselves and self-advancement. His model of high-road leadership consistently demonstrated that people matter most, not goals or agendas or preconceived expectations and outcomes. Jesus never complained about changing his plans, being interrupted, or focusing on the needs of others.

Simply put, high-road leadership requires us to treat others better than they treat us. That's what we're doing when we place people ahead of our agenda. We're serving people by following Jesus' example, giving others our best because we're grateful God has given us his best. Putting others ahead of ourselves and our agendas helps transform us into the kinds of people Jesus wants us to be.

Serving because you see people as valuable rather than as expendable commodities makes a huge difference. It shifts you from feeling like you are above them to putting yourself below them in order to lift them up. Changing your attitude changes your heart. Knowing God values someone and serving them for that reason makes serving others a joy.

When you serve others, you draw closer to Jesus and show him how much you love him. Every time you place others ahead of your agenda, you are serving Jesus. Such opportunities are both a privilege and a blessing. There may be no greater action you can take to become more like Jesus than placing people above your own agenda. When you make people your priority, you please Jesus and become a more loving, more impactful high-road leader.

CHECKING IN

Go around the group and check in by answering one or both of the following questions:

- What are some reasons we often overlook people when prioritizing goals and achievements?

- When have you recently experienced someone placing their agenda above your needs? How did you respond in that situation?

HEARING THE WORD

Have someone read aloud the following passage from Jesus' Sermon on the Mount:

"Here's another old saying that deserves a second look: 'Eye for eye, tooth for tooth.' Is that going to get us anywhere? Here's what I propose: 'Don't hit back at all.' If someone strikes you, stand there and take it. If someone drags you into court and sues for the shirt off your back, gift wrap your best coat and make a present of it. And if someone takes unfair advantage of you, use the occasion to practice the servant life. No more tit-for-tat stuff. Live generously.

"You're familiar with the old written law, 'Love your friend,' and its unwritten companion, 'Hate your enemy.' I'm challenging that. I'm telling you to love your enemies. Let them bring out the best in you, not the worst. When someone gives you a hard time, respond with the supple moves of prayer, for then you are working out of your true selves, your God-created selves. This is what God does. He gives his best—the sun to warm and the rain to nourish—to everyone, regardless: the good and bad, the nice and nasty. If all you do is love the lovable, do you expect a bonus? Anybody can do that. If you simply say hello to those who greet you, do you expect a medal? Any run-of-the-mill sinner does that.

"In a word, what I'm saying is, Grow up. You're kingdom subjects. Now live like it. Live out your God-created identity. Live generously and graciously toward others, the way God lives toward you."
Matthew 5:38–48, MSG

Now turn to the person next to you and share your answers to the following questions:

- How does treating people better than they treat you demonstrate the way God values them?

- Why is it easy to villainize others when they disrupt or interfere with your plans? What's required in order for you to demonstrate they are more important than your plans?

TAKING THE HIGH ROAD

Play the video segment for session 7. Using the space on the next page, note any big ideas that stand out to you or any questions you may have. Then take a few minutes with your group members to discuss what you just watched and explore these concepts in Scripture.

- Of the various ways Jesus prioritized people above his agenda, which ones stand out to you the most? Why do these resonate with you?

- Based on how Jesus interacted with people suffering from disease, injury, and impairment, what risks did he take to prioritize their healing?

- What can you learn about high-road leadership based on the way Jesus responded to those who criticized his willingness to put others first? How can his example help you put others above your own agendas?

94

NOTES

- Does putting others first come naturally or easily to you? Or do you tend to focus on results and the bottom line?

- Who are the people currently most in need of your time and attention? What obstacles and assumptions have prevented you from focusing on them?

LEADING LIKE JESUS

As this session winds down, complete the following short activity on your own.

Look over the video teaching notes you took or questions you had. Now reflect for a moment on the group discussion you just had and record any points you want to explore further or implement in your leadership style. Underline or circle anything you want to make sure you remember and reflect on prior to your next group session.

In the space below, complete the following sentences as you consider what you will take away from this session—including the teaching, activities, and discussions.

- The biggest challenge to putting people first for me is...

- One way I can remember to follow the example of Jesus and put others before my own agenda is...

CLOSING IN PRAYER

Share any personal prayer requests or updates you would like other group members to pray about, and then pray for those requests together, either silently or out loud or both. Give thanks for the times others have made you and your needs a priority, and ask God to open your eyes and ears to the people in need around you.

BEFORE NEXT TIME

Prior to your group's next meeting, conclude your reading of Jesus the High Road Leader by finishing Chapter 9, "Jesus Brought People Together." Begin reflecting on ways you can follow his example and unite people rather than causing division.

BETWEEN-SESSIONS PERSONAL STUDY

As you consider the way Jesus always put others above his own agenda, use the questions below to help you grow in this area of high-road leadership. Think through what needs to change in order for you to be more attuned to others and to prioritize their needs above your action plans and agendas. Begin with a few moments of silent prayer, stilling your heart before God and asking his Spirit to guide you as you engage with this next-to-last personal study.

CHOOSING THE HIGH ROAD

Leaders often get caught up in their own success, defining themselves by their title, authority, power, and privilege. High-road leaders, however, focus on serving others first—placing the needs of those around them before their own achievements and status. They take to heart what Jesus, the ultimate high-road leader, said: "Anyone who wants to be first must be the very last, and the servant of all" (Mark 9:35). This kind of servant-leadership requires continually placing people above your own agenda. That's what Jesus did throughout his time walking the earth and interacting with people.

We too easily forget that others must come first. We tend to want to elevate ourselves. We somehow think leadership should put us above others, even though Jesus didn't model that. Left unchecked, we slide to the low road, succumbing to false modesty and calculated staging to shape the way others see us. But our motives inevitably surface through the consistent pattern of our words and actions. When they are not aligned with what we say we believe, others notice and lose respect for us.

When we put people—all people—above our agendas as Jesus did, then our beliefs, actions, and words align. Others notice this as well and know that we genuinely care about them, earning their trust and respect for us. This was certainly the case with all kinds of people who encountered Jesus. Many sought out Christ because they felt valued and respected by him, seen and accepted no matter how culture and society labeled them. Jesus welcomed women and children, prostitutes and tax collectors, lepers and foreigners. Regardless of their gender, status, age, race, education, or role, everyone who encountered Jesus received respect, compassion, and understanding.

They were likely drawn to Jesus because He always gave them hope, not only in his actions, but with his words. He met their immediate needs in order to address their spiritual needs. Jesus said, "Who needs a doctor: the healthy or the sick? ... I'm here to invite outsiders..." (Matt. 9:12–13, MSG).

He told the Samaritan woman, who had quite a history of failed marriages, that he offered her living water that would quench the thirst in her soul: "Anyone who drinks the water that I give will never thirst—not ever" (John 4:14, MSG). In contrast to the enemy, who robs and kills and destroys, Jesus declared, "I came so they can have real and eternal life, more and better life than they ever dreamed of" (John 10:10, MSG).

When you value people above agendas, you not only meet their needs but give them hope —the hope found in trusting Jesus.

- Do you believe the temptation for self-promotion is greater for leaders? Why or why not?

- When has being a leader brought you certain perks and privileges? How have you handled the status, title, or attention that comes with those you lead?

- When have you been tempted to overlook others in order to focus on a goal or achievement you were pursuing? What have you learned about overcoming such temptations?

- When has your respect and trust grown because of the way someone valued you above their agenda? How did their example reflect the way Jesus related to others?

- How have you focused on the physical needs of others in order to point them to their spiritual need for Jesus? How does addressing others' physical needs often open an opportunity to address their spiritual needs?

LEADING BY GOD'S WORD

Interruptions and distractions tend to disrupt schedules and derail plans. They often pull you away from completing items on your to-do list and the productive results you expected to achieve. Many times, you may be tempted to view these as obstacles to be eliminated or problems with time management to be resolved. If you look at the life of Jesus, however, he never complained or expressed frustration when others pulled him away from what he was doing.

What you might view as an interruption, Jesus seemed to view as an opportunity. In fact, if you consider his life as recorded in the Gospels, you will notice that most of his ministry consisted of what appears to be interruptions. When faced with a choice between ignoring the needs of someone so that he could continue with his original plan, or pausing and placing someone else's needs ahead of an agenda, Jesus chose the latter. By paying attention to the present needs of others, Jesus showed that he valued people as his priority, not productivity.

We see this emerge when Jesus passed through the city of Jericho on his way to Jerusalem. Rather than rush to reach his destination, Jesus noticed one man in particular and intentionally made time to engage with him despite the criticism of others.

Jesus entered Jericho and was passing through. A man was there by the name of Zacchaeus; he was a chief tax collector and was wealthy. He wanted to see who Jesus was, but because he was short he could not see over the crowd. So he ran ahead and climbed a sycamore-fig tree to see him, since Jesus was coming that way.

When Jesus reached the spot, he looked up and said to him, "Zacchaeus, come down immediately. I must stay at your house today." So he came down at once and welcomed him gladly.

All the people saw this and began to mutter, "He has gone to be the guest of a sinner."

But Zacchaeus stood up and said to the Lord, "Look, Lord! Here and now I give half of my possessions to the poor, and if I have cheated anybody out of anything, I will pay back four times the amount."

Jesus said to him, "Today salvation has come to this house, because this man, too, is a son of Abraham. "For the Son of Man came to seek and to save the lost."
Luke 19:1–10

Jesus suspended his journey because Zacchaeus was eager to meet him, and Jesus realized the opportunity to spend time with a man who was financially wealthy but spiritually bankrupt. Jesus didn't care that others would criticize him. High-road leaders would rather do the right thing and be talked about poorly than to do the wrong thing and be praised. He wanted to see salvation come to Zacchaeus, and he did.

If we open our eyes and see the world the way Jesus did, we'll recognize that much of the ministry we can do in this life will consist of opportunities dressed up as interruptions. When God asks us to stop what we are doing, he is often giving us a chance to be a part of what he is doing. In God's kingdom, an interruption often becomes an invitation to do something better.

- How do you usually respond to interruptions in the course of a workday, especially a day in which your schedule is full?

- What strikes you about the way Jesus interacted with Zacchaeus? Why do you suppose Jesus not only made time for this man but invited himself to dine at Zacchaeus's house?

- How do you suppose most people treated Zacchaeus based on the details provided? Based on what he usually experienced, what do you think Zacchaeus expected when he saw Jesus walking toward his hiding place in the sycamore tree?

- When have you recently altered your schedule, travel plans, or meeting agenda in order to engage with someone in need? What did you learn from this experience?

>

- How does following the example set by Jesus force you to reconsider the way you set appointments, schedule meetings, and make plans?

>

WALKING THE HIGH ROAD

High-road leadership requires us to treat others better than they treat us. When we place people ahead of our agenda, we're following the example of Jesus by serving others. We're giving others our best because we're grateful God has given us his best. Motivated by gratitude and love, we grow into the kinds of people Jesus wants us to be. Rather than serving others out of duty or obligation, we discover how our hearts become more like the heart of Jesus, filled with respect, acceptance, and compassion for everyone we encounter.

This process does not usually happen immediately but shifts as we grow closer to Christ and become more willing to surrender our agenda and focus on his priority—people. Our attitude shifts from seeing others as a problem to be solved or a situation to be endured. Instead, we realize what a privilege we have to serve them and be Jesus to them. Serving because you see people as valuable shifts you from feeling like you are above them to putting yourself below them to lift them up. Changing your attitude changes your heart. Knowing how much God values someone and serving them for that reason makes serving others a joy.

Focusing on others and serving them acknowledges their worth and provides validation for their needs. When we put others above our own agenda, we communicate that they're more important than our schedule. It's as if we say, "There you are. I see you and care about you. How can I serve you?" This attitude lets them know they're important.

Only once did Jesus spell out that he was giving his disciples an example for them to follow. That was when he washed their feet. But that private experience of servanthood became a public experience. Jesus asked his followers to serve others in the same way. When people do that and discover the joy of seeing others valued and loved, they want to give that experience to others. Serving becomes contagious.

Washing his disciples' feet was not the only time Jesus made it clear that the way we treat others is important to him. Describing his future judgment of the sheep (those who followed him) and the goats (those who didn't), Jesus said he will invite his sheep to enjoy their eternal reward:

"'Take what's coming to you in this kingdom. It's been ready for you since the world's foundation. And here's why:

I was hungry and you fed me,

I was thirsty and you gave me a drink,

I was homeless and you gave me a room,

I was shivering and you gave me clothes,

I was sick and you stopped to visit,

I was in prison and you came to me.

"Then those 'sheep' are going to say, 'Master, what are you talking about? When did we ever see you hungry and feed you, thirsty and give you a drink? And when did we ever see you sick or in prison and come to you?' Then the King will say, 'I'm telling the solemn truth: Whenever you did one of these things to someone overlooked or ignored, that was me—you did it to me.'"

Matthew 25:35–40, MSG

Clearly, how you treat others matters. Jesus cares so much about how you treat others that he takes it personally. When you put people first and serve them, you're pleasing Jesus in ways you may not even be aware of. And Jesus will reward you in eternity for it. By serving others above your own agenda, you become more like him.

- When have you helped others because you knew you were supposed to, as opposed to helping others because you valued them? What caused the difference in your motivation?

- When have you recently been blessed by someone else's small gift of kindness toward you? How did their words, attitude, or action communicate that they valued you?

- How often do you view serving others as an opportunity to serve Jesus? How would you interact with others differently if you always saw them as a valuable child of God?

- When have you witnessed someone—perhaps a waitress, store clerk, or entry-level team member—being ignored or mistreated and intervened on their behalf? What message do you send to others when you treat "the least of these" as Jesus would treat them?

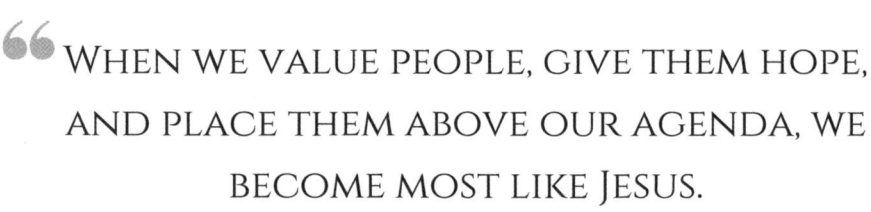
66 WHEN WE VALUE PEOPLE, GIVE THEM HOPE, AND PLACE THEM ABOVE OUR AGENDA, WE BECOME MOST LIKE JESUS.

JESUS THE HIGH ROAD LEADER, PAGE 153

SESSION 8
Jesus Brought People Together

In order to bring people together as Jesus did, we must remember our
goal is not to be right but to be in relationship.
Jesus the High Road Leader, page 173

GETTING STARTED

High-road leaders bring people together, and no one demonstrates this better than Jesus during his time on earth. He brought diverse people together in ways that continue to change our world. He never compromised truth to draw people together, and everything he did was fueled by grace. Jesus knew that some people would reject him and his radical message, that some would reject and persecute his followers, and yet he always sought to unite people with his Father and one another. Like every high-road leader, Jesus understood that bringing people together results in a powerful unity that is greater than the sum of its individuals.

You only need to look at the twelve people chosen by Jesus as his closest disciples for an example of his ability to unify diverse personalities. Among the twelve you will find down-to-earth, working-class fisherman such as Peter, James, and John (Matt. 4:18–22). There was Matthew, a tax collector (Matt. 9:9), an unpopular profession known for its corruption. And there was Simon the zealot (Matt. 10:4), a political revolutionary devoted to overthrowing the Romans and restoring Israel. These were not individuals who would probably hang out together if not for the one they all followed. Also notice that none of the disciples seems particularly well qualified for ministry. In fact, if you gave them personality tests or skill-set assessments, you probably wouldn't choose them to work together. Instead, however, Jesus poured his life into them, and they became unified as disciples and followers of Christ—and they changed the world.

Sadly, we live in a world today that seems to encourage and celebrate division. People are pressured to choose a side and focus on the differences between themselves and others—cultures, backgrounds, skin colors, religious beliefs, political positions, and worldviews—rather than connecting based on what they have in common. Too often, division relies on drawing a line between your side and the other side, between what you believe versus what others believe.

In order to bring people together as Jesus did, we must remember our goal is not to be right but to be in relationship. We are called to love as he loved. For us to have relationships with others, they must see and experience God's love through us—not just in what we say but by what we do. Jesus said, "A new command I give you: Love one another. As I have loved you, so you must love one another. By this all men will know that you are my disciples, if you love one another" (John 13:34–35).

Jesus is the ultimate high-road leader because he saw beyond the external differences and internal variations of the people he brought together, seeing it would allow them to sharpen one another and fulfill their potential. Jesus knew bringing people together frees them to be who God created them to be. We should invite people to come together for the same purpose.

CHECKING IN

Go around the group and check in by answering both of the following questions:

- Based on your experience, what's one thing that draws people together beyond their differences?

- What's one thing you have especially enjoyed about meeting for this group study? Why?

HEARING THE WORD

Have someone read aloud the following passage in which the apostle Paul describes how followers of Jesus can connect with others.

Though I am free and belong to no one, I have made myself a slave to everyone, to win as many as possible. To the Jews I became like a Jew, to win the Jews. To those under the law I became like one under the law (though I myself am not under the law), so as to win those under the law. To those not having the law I became like one not having the law (though I am not free from God's law but am under Christ's law), so as to win those not having the law. To the weak I became weak, to win the weak. I have become all things to all people so that by all possible means I might save some. I do all this for the sake of the gospel, that I may share in its blessings.
1 Corinthians 9:19–23

Pair up with someone and share your answers to the following questions:

- How would you summarize Paul's strategy for relating with others who are different than he is? What's his motivation?

How does finding common ground help you bring people together? What example comes to mind?

Taking the High Road

Play the final video segment, for session 8. Use the space on the next page to write down the big ideas you want to remember. Then take a few minutes with your group members to discuss what you just watched and explore these concepts in Scripture.

- How have you attempted to follow the example of Jesus by balancing truth and grace when relating to others? What have you learned from these times?

- What are some ways Jesus unified the twelve diverse people whom he chose as disciples? How did being a direct part of Jesus' ministry change them?

- When have you recently interacted with someone distinctively different from you in their beliefs? How did you resist the temptation to be right rather than to focus on relationship?

- Who do you often struggle to relate with? What areas of common ground do you share that you can use as a way to connect?

NOTES

- Do you agree that following the example of Jesus requires you to "connect before you correct"? Why or why not?

LEADING LIKE JESUS

As this session winds down, complete the following short activity on your own.

Briefly review the video teaching notes you took or comments you made. Reflect for a moment on the discussion you just had as well as previous group discussions. Write down any questions you want to answer or thoughts you want to explore further. Underline or circle anything you want to make sure you remember and reflect on now as your group completes this study.

In the space below, complete the following sentences as you consider what you will take away from this session as well as this entire study—including the teaching, activities, and discussions.

What I want to remember about the way Jesus brought people together is...

One way I can follow his example when interacting with others is...

One of my greatest takeaways from this entire group study would have to be...

CLOSING IN PRAYER

Go around the group and share any final personal prayer requests and updates you would like others to lift up, and then pray for those requests together, either silently or out loud or both. Thank God for each person in the group and the way you have learned and grown together as you seek to be more like Jesus. Ask him to bless your efforts to be a more loving, selfless high-road leader.

FINAL
PERSONAL STUDY

Now that you've completed reading and exploring Jesus the High Road Leader, use these final questions and exercises to help you reflect and evaluate your experience and all you've learned. To help with your time of reflection and assessment, you may want to review your previous answers, either flipping back in this guide or referring to the journal or notebook you used for your responses.

CHOOSING THE HIGH ROAD

So many people separate and divide others rather than bring them together and bless them. Jesus welcomed everyone and willingly extended his blessing to them, showing just how much he valued them. He knew that words have power to bring people together, as well as actions and attitudes. His example in various encounters with others demonstrates how you can unify and bless rather than divide and drive away.

1) Look for the Good in Every Person

Jesus saw the good in others even when they struggled to see it in themselves. While experiencing the agony of dying on the cross, Jesus recognized the faith expressed by the thief dying beside him. Instead of mocking Jesus as the other thief had done, this man pointed out, "We are punished justly, for we are getting what our deeds deserve. But this man has done nothing wrong.... Jesus, remember me when you come into your kingdom" (Luke 23:41–42). Jesus saw the good faith inside this man and responded, "Truly I tell you, today you will be with me in paradise" (Luke 23:43).

People are created in God's image, which means there is goodness in everyone. We can find it if we look for it, and we can let them know we see that goodness. We can remind others of how God sees and values them.

2) Express Your Gratitude to Everyone

Jesus frequently thanked his Father for providing both material items and spiritual power. Before blessing the loaves and fishes he would use to feed more than five thousand people, Jesus thanked God for the meager provision he used to perform a miracle (John 6:11). Before calling out his friend Lazarus from the tomb, Jesus thanked his Father for the ability to raise the dead (John 11:41). Jesus had an attitude of continual gratitude.

Giving thanks has the ability to bring people together because they feel seen, appreciated, and valued. Whenever you interact with others, don't overlook the impact that saying "thank you" and showing appreciation can have. If such gratitude positively impacts strangers and acquaintances, all the more reason to practice it with those who mean the most to you.

3) Let Everyone Know How Much You Care

Showing and expressing affection demonstrates our attunement to others' needs and lets people know how much we care. Jesus never hesitated to touch someone to heal them, although he could have done it by merely willing it. Nor did he pull away from people. During the last supper, John, the disciple whom Jesus loved, rested his head on his Master's chest (John 13:25).

We should not assume others know how much we care about them. We must be willing to tell them directly and show them in how we interact with them. When others know you care and value them, they want to be part of what you're doing.

4) Encourage Everyone You Meet

Encouragement is another powerful tool for bringing people together. Jesus encouraged people just with his presence and knew he gave them hope. But he also spoke specific words of encouragement to people to lift them up. For example, Jesus told his disciple, "And I tell you that you are Peter, and on this rock I will build my church, and the gates of Hades will not overcome it" (Matt. 16:18). And after his death and burial and resurrection, Jesus appeared to his disciples in the upper room where they had gathered to hide out from the Jewish authorities who might arrest them. He knew they were scared and anxious, and he greeted them with reassurance and encouragement, saying, "Peace be with you! As the Father has sent me, I am sending you" (John 20:21).

When you encourage others, you raise their courage to meet their need. Encouragement lets others know you can handle their struggles and boost them when they need it most. You can acknowledge someone's discouragement and help them see the bigger picture.

5) Show Kindness and Consideration in Every Situation

Kindness might seem like an obvious way to bring people together, but it is often surprisingly overlooked. Keep in mind, too, that kindness is not just being nice. Kindness is active and conveys safety, consideration, and compassion. You can see this in Jesus as our Good Shepherd, who pursues the one lost sheep that has wandered astray (Matt. 18:12–14).

Kindness, though gentle, is not weak or passive, but is intentional and powerful. The kindness modeled by Jesus reveals an attitude of grace present in every interaction, an extravagant generosity of going above and beyond, and the compassion of empathizing with people's needs, such as a short tax collector's curiosity or a sinful woman's shame. While condemnation and criticism will divide and separate, kindness as Jesus modeled it always brings people together.

6) Pray with and for Everyone You Can

Your willingness to talk to God about others shows how much you value them. And your heart gets right when you bring someone before the Father in prayer. It's hard not to love someone when you pray for them. Jesus prayed for children and blessed them (Matt. 19:13–14). He prayed for Simon during the Last Supper to protect him from Satan (Luke 22:31–32). And he prayed for all his followers the night before he went to the cross (John 17:9–18).

Our words are so powerful in their ability to unite and bring together. As high-road leaders like Jesus, we are called to bless and not to curse, to attract and not to repel. When you go out of your way to show everyone God's love, display grace in how you interact, and bless them, you will bring people together.

- Of the six ways listed to bring people together like Jesus did, which one do you already practice regularly? Which one do you need to be more intentional about practicing?

- How have others blessed and ministered to you through the ways described here? What recent examples come to mind?

- How often do you tell others how much you appreciate them and their efforts? How often do you show others your gratitude? Who needs to receive your appreciation today?

- What role has prayer played in your ability to bring people together? Who do you pray for regularly that does not know the Lord?

- How can you encourage those you serve today? Who needs to know that you see the good in them?

LEADING BY GOD'S WORD

You explored the idea of giving more than you take as a high-road principle back in Session 2. But consider how Jesus took that idea even further than simple generosity. He said, "You have heard that it was said, 'Love your neighbor and hate your enemy.' But I tell you: Love your enemies and pray for those who persecute you" (Matt. 5:43–44).

Not only are you to give more than you take—you are called to love those intent on harming you! This counterintuitive command reflects the kind of divine agape love that comes only from God. You can never love your enemies unless you have experienced God's love personally. Once you have experienced it, God expects nothing less than love for your enemies from you.

As if this notion weren't already radical enough, Jesus then ramped it up even more. Not only did he ask us to go the extra mile and turn the other cheek. Not only did he command us to love those who clearly do not love us. He asked us to bless them! Jesus said, "But to you who are listening I say: Love your enemies, do good to those who hate you, bless those who curse you, pray for those who mistreat you" (Luke 6:27–28).

Blessing someone not only means loving them but expressing this love with divine favor. It means to speak well of them and want the best for them. Blessing is the opposite of cursing and refuses to gossip or spread falsehoods. Peter admonished, "Do not do wrong to repay a wrong, and do not insult to repay an insult. But repay with a blessing, because you yourselves were called to do this so that you might receive a blessing" (1 Peter 3:9, NCV). Rather than giving someone what you, or they, might think they deserve, love them and bless them. Why? Because this is how God has loved you!

Blessing others not only signals to others that you see them but that you want God's divine favor for them. Others might not consider them worthy, but when you bless them, you remind them of how much God loves and values them. We find a beautiful illustration of this kind of blessing when Jesus welcomed the little children brought to him:

People were bringing little children to Jesus for him to place his hands on them, but the disciples rebuked them. When Jesus saw this, he was indignant. he said to them, "Let the little children come to Me, and do not hinder them, for the kingdom of God belongs to such as these. Truly I tell you, anyone who will not receive the kingdom of God like a little child will never enter it." And he took the children in his arms, placed his hands on them and blessed them.
Mark 10:13–16

Notice that the disciples tried to keep people away from Jesus instead of bringing them together. Perhaps they thought their master was too busy healing and preaching and teaching to bless a child. They might have been well-intentioned and didn't want Jesus to grow weary from the crowds following him. But Jesus insisted that the little children be allowed to come to him. Jesus not only blessed them but made it clear that we must be like them, earnest and eager, innocent and intent, if we want to be part of God's Kingdom.

- What are some ways you can bless those who oppose you or mean you harm? When have you been able to do this recently?

- Who is someone often considered unimportant or bothersome by others that you can intentionally bless with your words and actions? How can you bless them today?

- What stands out most to you in the interaction Jesus has with his disciples and the little children? Why?

- When has someone recently blessed you in some unexpected way? What impact did this have on you?

- What practices can you implement to regularly bless the people you lead and serve? What's one step you can take to bless them this week?

WALKING THE HIGH ROAD

Jesus was not simply trying to be a high-road leader for its own sake. If that's true, then why did he always travel the high road? Why did he value all people, never keep score, give more than he took, acknowledge his humanness, do the right things for the right reasons, embrace authenticity, place people above his agenda, and bring people together?

Jesus wanted to bring all of us back to God. Because sin created a chasm separating humankind from God, Jesus bridged that gap through his death on the cross. Jesus paid the price for our sin and transgressions: "But now in Christ Jesus you who once were far away have been brought near by the blood of Christ" (Eph. 2:13).

If you're committed to following Christ and growing in your faith, then you must follow the path Jesus calls you to travel. You must act in the same way Jesus, the ultimate high-road leader, did. You are called to bring people together and bring them to God. That has been his plan from the beginning. And it was Jesus himself who said, "Anyone who loves me will obey my teaching. My Father will love them, and we will come to them and make our home with them" (John 14:23).

It's relatively easy to exclude those who are different from you, condemn those who don't share your beliefs and personal faith, and overlook those outside your comfort zones. But that's not how Jesus acted. He always took the high road. He reached out to people who were different, engaged others with grace, and loved outsiders with compassionate connection.

As a high-road leader following his example, you can do these things too. Jesus has set the example for how you are to lead—by serving others because you're motivated by love. God has given you the Holy Spirit, so you always have the power to take the high road. And every day you receive new opportunities. The choice is yours to take.

As you look back over what you've learned and experienced, begin this final time of personal study by making a gratitude list, jotting down all the things that you especially appreciate from your time with the group, reading the book, and completing this study. Feel free to make your own list or use these prompts to get you started.

I am thankful for...

I give thanks to God especially for...

Thank you, Lord, for blessing me with...

What I really appreciate about the group is...

Look back through the notes, questions, and reflections you've written, both during your group meetings as well as between sessions. Then answer the following questions as you evaluate your experience during this study.

- *What stands out now from what you've written? Are there consistent themes or threads you see running throughout your experiences in the eight sessions?*

- *How has your relationship with God changed over the course of meeting with your group and completing this study? Where do you see evidence of this change in your notes, answers, and written reflections?*

- *How has the way you lead and serve others changed over the course of this study? What have you learned about being a Christlike high-road leader that wasn't clear to you before?*

- *What passage or verses from God's Word has empowered, encouraged, and inspired you the most as you follow the example of Jesus as a high-road leader? Why do you think this truth from the Bible means so much to you?*

117

Think back on each of your group's previous sessions and how they have shaped your thoughts. What do you know now that you didn't know then? Remember each group member and consider how they contributed to your overall experience in the group. Use the following questions to help you bring closure to this study, even as you carry your experience with you as you continue to follow Jesus and become more of a high-road leader.

- What stands out now from what you've written? Are there consistent themes or threads you see running throughout your experiences in the eight sessions?

- What surprised you most about your group experience completing this study? What disappointed you?

- What will you carry with you now that your group has concluded this study? How have you changed since starting and completing these sessions?

- Complete this sentence: "After this study, what I'll remember most can be summed up by this: _____."

"IN ORDER TO BRING PEOPLE TOGETHER AS JESUS DID, WE MUST REMEMBER OUR GOAL IS NOT TO BE RIGHT BUT TO BE IN RELATIONSHIP.

JESUS THE HIGH ROAD LEADER, PAGE 173

BONUS SESSION
THE FOUR PICTURES OF GOD

"I stand at the door and knock. If you hear my voice and open the door, I will come in..."

Revelation 3:20, NCV

GETTING STARTED

How you view things is how you do things.

If you are unable to see something accurately, then you naturally relate to it based on your misperception. Unfortunately, some of us have an inaccurate view of God that prevents us from knowing him and experiencing authentic relationship with him. These different perceptions of God can be described by four pictures. Three of these depict a wrong view of God, while one accurately illustrates the truth of who he is and how he views us.

The first wrong picture is a high, impenetrable wall. When some people think of God, they imagine this enormous, foreboding barrier. They're willing to acknowledge that there's probably a God, but they view him as removed and hidden behind this giant wall that keeps him unknowable. God is on the inside and they're forever on the outside, they falsely assume. They're unable to see that God wants relationship with them—he's not hiding behind a wall but rather coming to them through the bridge of his Son, Jesus.

The second faulty way of viewing God is a steep staircase going up to heaven. These people view God as up there while they're down here trying to work their way up to him step by step. They assume they have to work really hard to do the right things the right way in order to please God and come closer to him. They believe that if they can work and climb high enough, then just maybe they'll get close enough to know God. Religion often promotes this inaccurate way of viewing God by focusing on works and urging us to try harder.

The problem with this staircase to heaven is that we can never earn our way to God. We simply cannot be good enough long enough to advance toward him in relationship. The only way was for God to send his beloved only Son, Jesus, to earth to die for our sins. Praying in the Garden of Gethsemane on the night before he died, Jesus asked his Father if there was another way to accomplish relationship with people. Clearly, there was not—because we can never do enough on our own. Only Jesus could do it for us and offer us forgiveness of our sins and the free gift of salvation through his death on the cross.

The third faulty picture is a terrible one—a garbage dump or endless junkyard. Some people see all the mistakes they've made, all the messes they've created, all their failures and wonder why God would ever be interested in them. Because of all the garbage and junk spilling over in their life, they assume God could never forgive them and love them. Since they're often unwilling to forgive themselves, they mistakenly believe God would not forgive them either.

Not only is this not true—our failures and weaknesses reveal why Jesus came to save us! He said, "It is not the healthy who need a doctor, but the sick. I have not come to call the righteous, but sinners" (Mark 2:17). Jesus also referred to himself as the Good Shepherd relentless in his loving pursuit of lost sheep (Luke 15:4–7, John 10:11–18).

The accurate picture revealing how God relates to us is a door—the door of our heart. Jesus said, "Look! I stand at the door and knock. If you hear my voice and open the door, I will come in, and we will share a meal together as friends" (Rev. 3:20, NLT). Jesus will do anything in his power to come to you, but only you can open that door and invite him into your life. If you're 1,000 steps away from God, he will take 999 steps to get to you, but you must take the final step. Jesus loves you so much that he died for your sins so that you could experience abundant life in relationship with the Father.
Having an accurate view of God changes everything!

CHECKING IN

Go around the group and check in by answering both of the following questions:

- Which of the four pictures resonates with you most or illustrates how you view God and relate to him?

- What has influenced or contributed to your inaccurate views of God? What assumptions have you made about him based on inaccurate perceptions?

HEARING THE WORD

Have someone read aloud the following passage in which Jesus describes his love for the lost:

Then Jesus told them this parable: "Suppose one of you has a hundred sheep and loses one of them. Doesn't he leave the ninety-nine in the open country and go after the lost sheep until he finds it? And when he finds it, he joyfully puts it on his shoulders and goes home. Then he calls his friends and neighbors together and says, 'Rejoice with me; I have found my lost sheep.' I tell you that in the same way there will be more rejoicing in heaven over one sinner who repents than over ninety-nine righteous persons who do not need to repent."

Luke 15:3–7

Pair up with someone and share your answers to the following questions:

- How does this parable illustrate the way Jesus pursues those who are lost? Why is he willing to go to such great lengths to search for the lost sheep?

- When have you experienced the love of Jesus pursuing you during a time when you felt lost or had strayed from God?

TAKING THE HIGH ROAD

Play the final bonus video segment. Use the space below to write down the big ideas you want to remember. Then take a few minutes with your group members to discuss what you just watched and explore these concepts in Scripture.

NOTES:

_____

_____

_____

_____

- Who do you know that views God as hidden and unknowable behind a giant wall? How can you lovingly challenge their view with an accurate picture of how much God wants to know them?

- When have you found yourself trying to take the staircase approach to knowing God by doing more good works based on your own efforts? What have you learned about yourself and about God from such endeavors?

- What are some of the items in your personal garbage heap or junkyard that have made it challenging for you to see God accurately and believe he loves you and forgives you? How have you learned to see beyond your own mistakes and sinful shortcomings?

- When have you answered the knock at the door of your heart and invited Jesus into your life? If you haven't opened your heart and accepted Jesus into your life, are you willing to pray a prayer similar to the one John offers at the end of the video?

- What does it mean for Jesus not only to be your Lord and Savior but your friend and constant companion? When have you experienced this kind of spiritual intimacy with him?

LEADING LIKE JESUS

As this session winds down, complete the following short activity on your own.

Briefly review any video teaching notes you took or comments you made. Reflect for a moment on how you see God and how you currently relate to Jesus. Write down any questions you want to answer or thoughts you want to explore further. Underline or circle anything you want to make sure you remember and reflect on now as your group completes this study.

In the space below, complete the following sentences as you consider what you will take away from this bonus session.

What I will take away from this bonus session is...

I know that I have accepted Jesus into my heart because...

CLOSING IN PRAYER

Go around the group and share any remaining prayer requests and updates you would like others to lift up, and then pray for those requests together, either silently or out loud or both. Thank God for the gift of his Son, Jesus, and his limitless and unconditional love for you. Ask him to empower you to help others see him clearly so that they, too, might know how much he loves them and wants relationship with them.

66 TELL YOU THAT IN THE SAME WAY THERE
WILL BE MORE REJOICING IN HEAVEN OVER
ONE SINNER WHO REPENTS THAN OVER
NINETY-NINE RIGHTEOUS PERSONS WHO
DO NOT NEED TO REPENT.

LUKE 15:3–7

Thank you for agreeing to lead a small group through this study. What you have chosen to do is valuable and will make a great difference in the lives of others. Your leadership in the group study will reinforce many of the qualities of high-road leaders and allow participants to experience what they are learning.

Jesus the High Road Leader is an eight-session study built around video content and small-group interaction. As the group leader, just think of yourself as the host of a dinner party. Your job is to take care of your guests by managing all the behind-the-scenes details so that when everyone arrives, they can just enjoy time together.

As the group leader, your role is not to answer all the questions or re-teach the content—the video, book, and study guide will do most of that work. Your job is to guide the experience and create an environment where people can process, question, and reflect—not receive more instruction.

Make sure everyone in the group gets a copy of the study guide along with the book, Jesus the High Road Leader. This will keep everyone on the same page and help the process run more smoothly. If some group members are unable to purchase the guide, arrange it so that people can share the resource with other group members. Giving everyone access to all the material will position this study to be as rewarding an experience as possible. Everyone should feel free to write in their study guides and bring them to group every week.

SETTING UP YOUR GROUP

As the group leader, you'll want to create an environment that encourages sharing and learning. A church sanctuary or formal classroom may not be as ideal as a living room, because those locations can feel formal and less intimate. No matter what setting you choose, provide enough comfortable seating for everyone, and, if possible, arrange the seats in a semicircle so everyone can see the video easily. This will make transition between the video and group conversation more efficient and natural.

Also, try to get to the meeting site early so you can greet participants as they arrive. Simple refreshments create a welcoming atmosphere and can be a wonderful addition to a group study evening. Try to take food and pet allergies into account to make your guests as comfortable as possible. You may also want to consider offering childcare to couples with children who want to attend. Finally, be sure your media technology is working properly. Managing these details up front will make the rest of your group experience flow smoothly and provide a welcoming space in which to engage the content of Jesus the High Road Leader.

LEADER'S GUIDE

STARTING YOUR GROUP TIME

Once everyone has arrived, it's time to begin the group. Here are some simple tips to make your group time healthy, enjoyable, and effective.

First, consider beginning the meeting with a short prayer, and remind the group members to put their phones on silent. This is a way to make sure you can all be present with one another and with God. Then, give each person one or two minutes to respond to the questions in the "Checking In" section. You won't need much time in session 1, but beginning in session 2, people may need more time to share as you all get better acquainted. Usually, you won't answer the discussion questions yourself, but you may need to go first a couple of times and set an example, answering briefly and with a reasonable amount of transparency.

At the end of session 1, invite the group members to complete the Between-Sessions personal studies for that week. Let them know that it's not a problem if they can't get to some of the between-sessions activities some weeks. It will still be beneficial for them to do what they can as they process and implement what they're learning in the group.

LEADING THE DISCUSSION TIME

Now that the group is engaged, it's time to watch the video and respond with some directed small-group discussion. Encourage all the group members to participate in the discussion, but make sure they know they don't have to do so. As the discussion progresses, you may want to follow up with comments such as, "Tell me more about that," or, "Why did you answer that way?" This will allow the group participants to deepen their reflections and invite meaningful sharing in a nonthreatening way.

Note that you have been given multiple questions to use in each session, and you do not have to use them all or even follow them in order. Feel free to pick and choose questions based on either the needs of your group or how the conversation is flowing. Also, don't be afraid of silence. Offering a question and allowing up to thirty seconds of silence is okay. It allows people space to think about how they want to respond and also gives them time to do so.

As group leader, you are the boundary keeper for your group. Do not let anyone (yourself included) dominate the group time. Keep an eye out for group members who might be tempted to "attack" folks they disagree with or try to "fix" those having struggles. These kinds of behaviors can derail a group's momentum, so they need to be steered in a different direction. Model active listening and encourage everyone in your group to do the same. This will make your group time a safe space and create a positive community.

The group discussion time leads to a closing individual activity. During this time, encourage the participants to take just a few minutes to review what they've learned and write down a few key takeaways. This will help them cement the big ideas in their minds as you bring the session to an end. Close your time together with prayer as a group.